Country Ways

in Kent

From Gwen

Christmas 1986

Other titles in this series:
Country Ways in Hampshire & Dorset
Country Ways in Sussex & Surrey

Country Ways

in Kent

ANTHONY HOWARD

Countryside Books/TVS

First Published 1986
© Text Anthony Howard 1986

Countryside Books
3 Catherine Road,
Newbury, Berkshire.

ISBN 0 905392 67 1

Front Cover Photograph: Aquila Photographics
Back Cover Photograph: Derek Budd

Photographs by Derek Budd, Tony Nutley and Tim Sharman

Produced through MRM (Print Consultants) Ltd, Reading
Typeset by Acorn Bookwork, Salisbury
Printed in England by Borcombe Printers, Romsey

CONTENTS

INTRODUCTION

The Lowes were in their eighties. They lived an independent life in a simple two up and two down cottage with five acres, at the top of a muddy track. They grew all their own vegetables and kept rabbits to eat. At five o'clock each morning you could hear the 'ping, ping, ping' of Mr. Lowe hammering in posts to tie up the goats for the day after milking. The floors of their home were earthy and uneven. The garden was wild and used only for practical things. They managed without a fridge or running water, and mostly they cooked on an open fire. They were fine, proud people, content with their lot, and they staunchly resisted the attempts of social workers and politicians to interfere with and change the way of life they had chosen. Through their grandparents they had memories which went back to the 18th century, and they would entertain the village children with stories of ancient milk-rounds, of harvest festivals after the corn had all been scythed, stooked and stacked and of the last man to be hanged from the village oak — tales of a rural England that is past and largely forgotten.

Country Ways attempts to capture some of the personal history of people like the Lowes before it disappears forever. It may be that modern life in England is cleaner, faster and more comfortable for most people, but who will argue that it is more contented, safer or more cheerful?

There are stark contrasts in the county of Kent between town and country, ancient and modern, wild and tame places. Places such as Thanet, Ashford and Maidstone have been changed greatly by the needs of 20th century life, though Canterbury and the Garden of England retain much that is admirable.

And there always remains the glory of much of the lovely coastline, the fertility of the Weald and the beauty of the oast houses and the old smugglers' inns.

Marion Studd feeding lambs on her farm at Eastchurch on the Isle of Sheppey, where her great-grandfather and grandfather farmed before her.

A master of the silent attack, the tawny owl is a highly specialised nocturnal hunter with exceptional hearing and sensitive vision.

The Romney Marsh has a special magical quality with its windswept plains and dykes.

ROMNEY MARSH

WHEN the wind elbows its way through the tall banks of rushes on the Romney Marsh, it is like the noise of a thousand anxious people whispering to one another in the language of the snakes. This is the sound of the marshland – a strange beak of land on the south coast of Kent pointing out into the Channel towards France. It is a mysterious, windswept plain, and the sigh of the sea-breezes in the reeds along the dykes – known locally as sewers – is as characteristic as the fog, which penetrates and cloaks the flatlands like a widow's weeds when the wind falls.

The real Marsh folk are a breed peculiar to the place itself. Some of them can trace their ancestry back through the days of smugglers and excisemen to the Roman legions, which first set foot on British soil on the shores of Romney Marsh. And their best-known sport – hare coursing, for which the table-flat fields of the area are ideally suited – was brought over by Roman soldiers, who had inherited it down the centuries from the Ancient Egyptians.

Strangers are welcome on the Marsh until they begin to interfere. It is said that 'All Marsh folk has been smugglers since time everlastin'', and it is perhaps a legacy of those smuggling days that the inhabitants of the towns and villages are proud, fiercely independent, secretive and disdainful to inquisitive questioners.

It must have been the wind-torn, desolate, reed-blown, melancholy, magical quality of the place, which prompted Kipling to have one of his characters describe the Marsh in terms verging on megalomania – 'There are six continents in the world – Asia, Africa, Europe, the Americas, Australia and the Romney Marsh.'

The waves that thunder ashore at Dungeness are the waves which brought the Roman armies to England. But for over two thousand years before the Romans, the Marsh was covered by primaeval forest. Sometime between then and the arrival of Caesar's centurions the sea overwhelmed the entire area one fearful, flooding night, and the high land, which today stands to the north of Romney Marsh, became the cliffs along the Channel sea coast. It is this constant battle for survival with the invading sea that gives the marshland its unique atmosphere and character. Even today, as the tides ebb, the waterways begin to empty their burden into the sea and, as the tide begins to flow, the water gates in the sea walls are firmly closed by the pressure of the salt water and the marshland is secure again, until the arrival of another monster sea powerful enough to foil the ingenuity even of modern man.

All through history the Romney Marsh has left its mark on great events, and history has left its distinctive signs on the Marsh. Ancient churches and castles abound. Lympne was once a Roman watch tower and the stony ruins below it were fortifications to protect the invading army. The peaceful church at New Romney with high water rings on its mighty columns still bears witness to another flood, which swept across the Marsh over 700 years ago. Camber Castle was built by Henry VIII against a threatened invasion by the Pope.

The Royal Military Canal was dug as a first line of defence against the possibility of Napoleon using the same route as the Romans for his projected invasion. Even the fortifications built during the Second World War have left their scar on the face of the Marsh. And there is evidence too of its reluctant entry into the nuclear age with the monstrous power station at Dungeness.

THERE can be few places in the world so profoundly and so wantonly touched by so many centuries of human history. But it is the people of the Marsh who have dictated the character of the place. They have remained significantly unchanged for generations. One of them is farrier and blacksmith, Robert Tanner. He is also a budding show-jumper. His smithy is between Lydd and Dungeness, and he exercises his horses on the Dungeness sands at low-tide. His family goes back for centuries on the Romney Marsh.

'It's the sort of place that grows on you. I've been here all me life – born and bred on the Marsh – and, I dunno, it's a place all of its own. Everywhere else is a foreign country. This is home. Where else can you come on a space like this? It's all open. It's all free. There's nobody going to chase you. There's nothing you can damage down 'ere – only yourself – and that's that. It's quite unique.'

Robert canters his favourite horse along the sands as the waves uncoil on the beach. The little fishing huts give the place the look of a city allotment, built on a field of stones. Masts of beached boats lean at crazy angles and strange seaweeds thrust their way through the shingle. Robert turns and heads for home and for his day's work. Soon his strong, dark figure is lit up by the glow of red-hot coal as the bellows roar, the anvil rings and the iron is tamed for today's customers.

'The more you know about horses – the firmer grounding you've got with them – the better blacksmith that you're going to make. The best blacksmith is the best-trained blacksmith. There's a lot more to it than just nailing on bits of iron. I mean, you're talking about live flesh there. All horses are different. Each one has got a different temper. You've gotta know which are the bad ones and which are the good ones, which ones are going to try and kill yer, which ones are just nervous and frightened of you. You're virtually got to be a psychiatrist to work 'em all out.'

The hours which Robert has to work today are not as long as they were for his predecessors. But he is still off in his van from before dawn until after dusk, looking after the hooves of the local horses.

'I learnt my trade from an old blacksmith on the Marsh called Jim Roach. His family had been in blacksmithying something like 400 years from father to son. He was one of the real old school. Dead straight and a different type of character. He was always telling us about how cart horses used to come to the forge at four o'clock in the morning, and you'd have to shoe three or four of them before you could have any breakfast.

'And then, if the farmers were getting busy, you didn't get any breakfast at all. You had to keep going until all the horses were done. It was a lot harder life in those early days with the bigger 'orses. They were working 'orses. It was a different trade then to what it is now. But, even today, as far back as I can remember it's just been 'orse after 'orse after 'orse.' The sparks fly and that unmistakable smell of burning hoof wafts across a Marsh meadow as Robert shoes a young girl's pony beside a shabby, lean-to stable.

FOX hunting and hare-coursing – the centuries-old field-sports of the Romney Marsh – are still popular pastimes in the area. Both are wrapped in controversy and, as a result, local people are unwilling to discuss them with strangers. The experts have an unerring instinct for where the hares or foxes will run to try to escape from the pursuing hounds. Even on a weekday, as many as forty riders turn out for the meets of the East Kent Hunt, and a great many more come on foot, bicycle and in motor-cars. A lot of the horses have been tended by Robert Tanner. Farmer Harold Crump is dedicated to fox-hunting, and has been farming on the Marsh all his life.

The country across which horses, hounds and foxes work is wonderfully fertile corn, potato and grazing land. The major industry on the Marsh is agriculture. The old Marsh farmers are bitter at what they see as the invasion from Lincolnshire of ambitious and ruthless men, who they say tore the heart out of that county and, when erosion took its toll, came to the Romney Marsh, where they ploughed up the grazing land to grow cash crops. Some of the old men say that these new farmers will eventually leave the Marsh in the same state as they left the fenland. And certainly there is far less grazing than there once was. Harold Crump has a long memory.

'We didn't hunt much on the Marsh pre-war. But then the East Kent had a Master farming down here and, in 1946, we started hunting here regularly. It's not that good this early in the season. It's best from January. We were once an all-farmer hunt. We've still got quite a sprinkling today. But it's changed a lot and we don't seem to be getting so many of the younger generation for some unknown reason. I suppose there's other alternatives for them.'

Whatever the arguments for and against fox-hunting, there is no denying that it is a colourful and traditional country scene. In the low-lying mist the horses and riders look like a troop of Victorian cavalry, and the pink coats of the huntsmen provide a bright splash of colour in the drab winter landscape. The sounds of muffled horns and iron shoes on metalled roads help recapture an atmosphere, which has remained largely unchanged for generations.

'When we were boys we didn't dress up in pink. We just wore breeches or leggings or ordinary clothes. It was the upper class that wore the pink. Now it's changed completely. In those days we rode any old, cheap horse that we could lay our hands on. People say it's cruel. But there's another side to that. The number of times we catch a fox with a wire round his middle or which has been shot and peppered is nobody's business. So, in my view, we're doing a good job, 'cos we're catching any damaged or weaker ones, and acting as a balance to nature.' And Harold canters off into the distance to join the rest of the riders, and the hounds, which, in spite of the lack of excitement, are still going strong.

ALEX Johnson is a merry Yorkshireman with kind eyes and a friendly smile. His favourite day out is to go hare-coursing with his lurcher. He lives in isolation in a caravan in a remote corner of the Marsh. He makes his living dealing in scrap metal and, in the season, picking fruit. Alex came to Kent through the Army. He was demobbed from the School of Infantry at Hythe, married the daughter of one of the oldest families there and has stayed ever since.

'I like the area. It's warmer for a start. It's two overcoats warmer than it is up Yorkshire – probably three. It might seem bleak here to someone who has been used to towns. But it isn't bleak to me. And you can earn a living. I wouldn't turn round and say you can earn a fortune. But it depends what type of life you want. You can't have everything, can you? And we've got fresh air and peace – and there's a lot can't say as much.'

Unlike most countrymen Alex is sentimental about animals. There are three contented donkeys in his small scrubby meadow. 'I've had them about six months. I went up to Ashford Market to buy another 'orse, and I see these three donkeys – the only ones that were in that day. And I thought, "They look nice". There was only one other bloke bidding for them. He was the dog-meat man. So I thought, "If they don't go too dear, I'll buy 'em." So I gave them thirty-five quid a piece for 'em. That was a bit dearer than what they'd fetch for meat. So they were saved. I think I'll put them on the beach to earn their livings in the summer.'

Alex is content with his way of life on the Marsh. 'It may not be everyone's cup of tea. But I can make a go of collecting junk – rags and any sort of old metal. It's all what I've ever done all me life. It's a living. Then, in the summer, we do fruit-picking. There's strawberry-picking and a bit of apple-picking; anything that's going. And, of course, it gives a break from collecting scrap in the winter. Because you can't keep going round collecting junk. There's only so much of it. Once they've turfed it out in the winter, it takes all summer to build it up again, dunnit? I meet all sorts of people – from the Lord of the Manor down to the ordinary chap in the street. I find that you can always do a good deal with the Lord of the Manor 'cos they seem to live and let live. Like where I come from up Yorkshire. They're always talking about the self-made man. But they're the worst ones to deal with. Probably, if I had plenty of money and had come up the hard way, if a chap come to buy summat off of me, I'd

14

want the last shilling. But the Lord of the Manor, he always seems to give you a good crack of the whip. No, I like the Marsh. I've been kicking about here since 1955 when it was all sheep. Now the Lincolnshire farmers have come down and turned it into arable land. But I still can't see that it'll ever change that much. The people don't change anyway.' And nor does Alex, who seems to be as unchanging as the seasons themselves.

ONE of the ancient and solemn traditions of the Romney Marsh is The Liberty, a gathering which dates back to 1462 and the reign of King Edward IV. It is made up of the Bailiff, 24 Jurats and the Commonalty or ordinary people of the area. The Jurats are a self-electing body, but the meetings of The Liberty can be attended by anyone who lives in the Romney Marsh area. The Bailiff also sits on The Level, another group of marshmen, whose origins vanish in the mists of antiquity and who were once responsible for the vital sea defences and drainage of the Marsh.

The Liberty once had supreme power over the running of the Marsh. But this authority disappeared with the Judicature Act of 1949, when they lost the right to appoint magistrates and to hold their own Court. In their day they had almost unlimited jurisdiction over debts, accounts, covenants, contracts, trespasses, arms, charters and every other activity on the Marsh.

Today, the meetings of the Liberty are purely for traditional and ceremonial reasons. But it would be foolish to underestimate the social and political influence of a group of people wedded together by their love of the Romney Marsh and their loyalty to its close-knit community. And the gaol outside the meeting hall, which now only houses wine left behind by some dear, departed vicar of Dymchurch, bears testimony to the days when the Liberty's powers were practical and unfettered and when many a villain or smuggler awaited his savage punishment there.

Even today, if you go into a Romney Marsh Inn and ask about smuggling, eyes harden and voices fall. A tradition as long as this one does not die easily. There are stories of fish stuffed with diamonds in marked boxes, and rumours of packages being dropped off ships as they pass close to Dungeness Point, and of powerful cars with winking lights parked in narrow lanes, while men change out of wet-suits. Whatever the truth of such stories, smuggling has been an integral and formative part of the life of the Marsh.

WHEREVER there are horses, there is leather and saddlery. Horses are much in evidence on the Romney Marsh, both for pleasure and as a means of transport. David Radley, whose little workshop is just above the Marsh at Mersham, is responsible for the upkeep and manufacture of harness for many of the Marsh ponies. He also repairs old carriages and pony traps. 'I first learnt the trade in London. I started there on a six week trial and found that I enjoyed the work so much that I've been doing it ever since – nearly 25 years now.'

David's strong fingers work at the tough leather, and rows of spikes and hammers

David Radley makes and repairs saddles and harness at his workshop at Mersham. He also keeps alive the craft of carriage and trap renovation.

and all the other tools of his trade hang on the wall beside him. Cut-outs of saddles and stacks of uncut leather lie on a second work-bench, and tins of needles and thread and knives and scissors are ranged nearby. Sometimes David is asked to cater for creatures other than horses.

'It was April 1st of all days. The phone rang. It was the vet at Howletts Zoo asking whether we could make a boot for his rhinoceros. It had an abscess on the bottom of its foot and when they cut the abscess out, you could have put a golf-ball in it. Well, I'd never seen a rhino's foot. I didn't really know what shape it was. But we reckoned that it would be round. The first boot we fitted, the rhinoceros stood against his concrete water trough and just kicked it to pieces. So we went back to the drawing-board. By then we had found out that his foot was more like the shape of a horseshoe. So we made one to a different design and a little bit stronger and fitted that. Luckily, he was happy with that one and he wore it for fourteen days. His foot healed up and the boot is now in the museum at the zoo.'

David has only once been to a tannery and he is honest enough to admit that he found the smell quite sickening. But that experience has not put him off working with leather, especially when it comes to restoring beautiful, old horse-drawn vehicles, which gleam gold and blue and brown in a nearby workshop.

'It's the most rewarding thing of all to see a carriage when it's really dilapidated, to see it stripped down to the bare wood and then rebuilt, repainted, releathered and to come out looking as good as it was when it was first made.' As long as there are dedicated craftsmen like David Radley around, the old skills will not die out.

IN days gone by the Romney Marsh farmers used to drive their sheep along the lanes to the lamb sales at Ashford Market. Nowadays it is the job of the hauliers. Tough work for people like Kathy Scamp who humps bales, loads cattle and sheep and drives her enormous lorry with the best of them.

'I suppose it is a strange life for a woman, but I don't see it that way, because I've always done it. It's a hard life really but I'm used to it so perhaps I don't notice it. It's a transport job as much as anything – loading up cattle and sheep from here and there and taking them somewhere else – markets and sales yards and the like. But I also deal a bit. I go out and buy a few bullocks, or even saddles and bridles and that sort of thing – anything that'll sell again.'

Kathy is strong and tough. In her sweater and heavy boots she takes on jobs and lifts loads at which many men would balk. But she is also very gentle and a little sentimental. 'Every day I have to go and look at my cattle. I've got some in Ashford and all around – not just at my place. I've got quite a bit of land about – some of it rented. But my cows at my home, I wouldn't sell those. When they get too old and have to be sold I load them up here and I take them straight to a slaughter-house. It's horrible. It worries me a lot. If they get very old, there comes a point when you're being cruel. But I do get fond of them and sometimes I think I'm daft and so soft that I shouldn't be in this job. But there it is.'

17

Ashford Market on the day of a lamb sale is a sea of woolly backs, and a bustling meeting place for friends and farmers from all over the Romney Marsh and from every part of Kent. Hard business is done, of course. Deals are struck. Bargains are made. But there is also the exchange of information, the making of contacts and the pleasure of the company of the likes of Kathy Scamp.

'During the autumn and up until nearly Christmas we have a lamb sale most Fridays. People come from all over the place. They might buy as many as three or four hundred sheep. There are a lot of really good characters at the market – real farming types. But, of course, a lot of the old dealers have gone now unfortunately – you know, passed over. I love cattle and horses. I love any livestock really. I love the countryside. And, of course, living on the edge of the Romney marsh. I love it above all.'

PEOPLE on the Romney Marsh often say to visitors – 'You either love it here or you hate it. We love it.' It sometimes sounds like a challenge. And there is something solid and defensive about this close-knit, unique community. Perhaps it's a characteristic which traces itself back to smuggling days when groups of desperate men roamed the area and often murdered and brutalised the population. The members of the hated Hawkhurst Gang were seen, after a successful cross-channel run, in the Mermaid Inn at Rye 'carousing and smoking their pipes with their loaded pistols on the table before them, no magistrate daring to interfere with them'.

The churches, pubs, ponds, cellars, ditches and cottages of the Marsh are still marked by traces of hiding places for barrels of brandy and other booty. Smugglers were thugs, but they were perhaps more acceptable to the people of the Marsh than the press gangs, the soldiers, customs officers and Preventivemen, who were often equally cruel. It was a bitter choice between two evils.

18

GARDEN OF ENGLAND

THE first railway came to Kent in 1830, and the transformation of much of the county into commuter-land started soon afterwards. The tide of extravagance flowed deep into the beautiful countryside. But in spite of the corrupting influence of wealthy newcomers, the central part of the county has managed to retain, with pride and with some justice, the title of 'The Garden of England'. There are other lovely counties in Britain, where this description is profoundly resented. But anyone who has seen the orchards, the hop-gardens and the pastures of mid-Kent in their full bloom can hardly quarrel with the picture of a beautiful, fertile garden.

In *A Boy in Kent*, C. Henry Warren recalled the feudalism in his Kentish village at the end of the last century. There was, for instance, a Jacob's ladder of social distinction in church. 'The higher up we were, the nearer we were to God.' Last to arrive for morning service and nearest to the altar was the Lady of the Manor and 'not until she was seated did the vicar dare to come out of the vestry'. Although much of the feudalism has vanished today, traces of its existence still remain in the grand homes and trim villages, and in the sweeping acres of rich farms. But the people themselves seem quiet and modest – a pleasant contrast to their noisy London neighbours to the north.

London, of course, has been directly responsible for nurturing the Garden of England. It provides a voracious and nearby market-place for the produce of the Kent orchards and market-gardens. Strawberries in season, flowers, apples and pears and every other kind of fruit, cob-nuts and cherries flowed and continue to flow into the Capital. In the opposite direction, a migrant labour-force of up to 65,000 hop-pickers used to travel from London into Kent during the early autumn, and they left their own indelible, cockney mark on the county. By the end of the 19th century, some of the agricultural methods, which we consider to be relatively modern, had already been adopted by Kent's fruit-farmers: intensive feeding, grading, packing, storing, pick-your-own fruit and selling produce to jam factories.

FOUR generations of John Paine's family have lived in Kent. He was born in 1914 and can just remember the Zeppelins gliding overhead. Bearded and benign he lives in a remote cottage near East Sutton. He used to farm fruit and hops, about which he is an international expert and adviser. Today he is left with his sheep and his memories, and the joys of living in the Garden of England. 'My home is on the greensand. This is very fertile soil mixed with clay, which holds the water. So we never suffer from drought.'

John strides away through an apple orchard to look over his flock of Kent ewes and lambs. His sheep-dog follows closely at his heels. The sun shines through the branches and autumn birds sing. 'These sheep come from the Romney Marsh. They're unique because they can live closely together on a small bit of land. We cross them with a Suffolk ram because the people who buy the lambs prefer a Suffolk-cross lamb from a Kent ewe. I've got 125 lambs and they're going to be sold on Friday in the store market. They'll go away to Oxford or to the Welsh markets for keeping over the winter.'

With the help of an old, retired shepherd, John Paine separates ewes and lambs, trims feet, doses, examines and checks his flock. The sheep-dog seems to be everywhere at once. It jumps fences three times its own height with the greatest of ease. To the anxious sheep it must seem that there are half a dozen bustling collies. 'The breeding ewes and rams I keep all the time. They stay till they get to old age. Then they go away to market and down to the Marsh, where they'll have one more successful lambing season, which they wouldn't have if they stayed up here. Most sheep come to the end of their useful life because their teeth wear out – in fact, they usually drop out. If somebody could invent an economical way of providing sheep with false teeth they would go on for another five, six or seven years!'

The ferile farmland stretches away and gleams in the October sunshine. Distant churches, oasts and small clumps of woodland break the sky-line. The fields and hedges are alive with birds and wild-life. A particularly bold grey squirrel gallops across the ploughed land more than a hundred yards from the safety of the nearest tree. 'All around are the remains of the Forest of Andrieda, which used to cover the whole of the Weald. One of the interesting things that has remained from those far-off days is the vermin hedge, which stretches across the back of the land. All the wild animals go from one piece of Forest to another up the vermin hedge, following the same track that has been used for centuries. This was a favourite place for the old-time gamekeepers, who used to set their traps to catch the stoats and weasels. The stoats would eat the young pheasants and the weasels would eat the pheasants' eggs. So, of course, the keepers wanted to get rid of them. They had a special place where they would hang up the corpses of everything they caught. When I was a boy I would go there and find dead sparrowhawks, kestrels, owls, stoats, weasels, jays and magpies hanging in rows. Now some of those creatures, like the sparrowhawk, are almost never seen here. The kestrels have gone to the motorways, where they can find plenty of freshly-killed food. And so tremendous changes have occurred in my lifetime in the wild-life of this old Forest.'

John turns back to his sheep and his preparations for Friday's market. His mind and his eyes are on his work but, like all true countrymen, he does not miss any movement in the surrounding fields and hedges. And it is from this constant attention that his knowledge and his wisdom come.

John Paine from East Sutton with one of his lambs which he breeds from Kent ewes and Sussex rams. His family have lived in Kent for four generations.

With his sons, Stanley Tassell farms in the valley of the owls in the heart of the Kentish orchards and hop fields.

OCTOBER is the end of the apple harvest in the Garden of England. Growing fruit for today's choosy and demanding markets, where customers seem to want apples which look as though they have been produced from a standard mould, is a skilled profession, depending heavily on years of experience and hard and meticulous work. Stanley Tassell and his three sons farm together at Ulcombe – the Valley of the Owls – with a magnificent view in fine weather across the Kentish orchards and hop fields.

'My father had the farm before me. He started in 1924 and we've been growing apples ever since. Then eventually he died and that was it. You suddenly find that you're in at the deep end doing all that he used to be doing. And the rewards are there too. When I look out of my bedroom window and see all the farm, all the way across the fields, it's a fine feeling and a jolly good view in the evenings when it's cool.'

Like many farmers Stanley Tassell does not rush at you with his words. He weighs his words and thinks before he talks. 'We're lucky. Our land is good. We've got some heavy clay soil at the bottom of the village. We grow cereals down there. But up on this land it's strawberries and apples. This used to be a hop-garden, but we gave up hops about twenty years ago.'

Tractors drive up and down between the rows of apple-trees, weighed down with impossible amounts of perfect fruit. Pretty girls pick the apples, and the tractors carry the huge wooden crates, filled to overflowing, back to the farmyard. 'It's taken us nine years to get a decent crop from these trees. But we're just starting to plant another root stock, which should come in in about three years. These trees will go on for another twenty years. We've just finished picking the Cox's Orange Pippins. That was a very good crop. We used to pick them into wooden carriers years ago – we'd buy them from the blind people, who made them. But now we've gone over to aluminium picking baskets. The basket can't close up with the weight of the fruit and that stops the bruising. That's the theory at any rate.'

Up at the barn the crates of apples are unloaded onto a massive moving belt which carries them under a broad and heavy shower-bath. High on the ceiling of the barn is stored all the old equipment, which was used in Stanley's childhood. 'I can remember riding on the van that collected the fruit. It was all wicker baskets in those days. They're not used nowadays of course. And we've got a ladder up there with 54 treads, and the men used to put that up into the cherry trees. 54 steps – that's a terrific height. That's when trees were big and men were strong. Yes, things have changed a lot now. The apples go straight into cold-store and pack house, and they have to be dipped in chemicals to stop any rotting. If there's an apple that's gone and there's the slightest rot, it rots its neighbours as well. So we dip them in chemicals to stop that. But I still enjoy the apples, although my boys would rather have the corn.'

ALTHOUGH Stanley Tassell farms the Valley of the Owls, it is rare nowadays to find 'the silent killers with feathers muffled in velvet' in the area. But at East Farleigh Alan Gardiner's home is a haven for wild-life of every kind, and his speciality is giving shelter and treatment to lost and injured owls. Alan handles the owls without fear and often without gloves. They sit quietly on his hand as he stands in the shade of a tall beech tree in his peaceful garden. On the opposite hill are the pointed cowls of a working oast.

'This Short-eared owl is a daylight-hunting owl. It came to me with a damaged wing. By the time that a bird has been down on the ground for a while with a broken wing, it has got filthy and lost a lot of weight. I don't normally keep them then. But this is such a lovely bird that I hung onto it.'

The next owl is clearly in an ugly mood, and Alan hurries indoors to get a stout leather glove before he picks it up. 'We've got a very angry owl here. It's a long-eared owl. You can see the ears quite clearly. It's a woodland bird – one of the two owls which hoot. Everyone thinks that owls hoot, but most of them don't. They hiss and scream and click a lot. But this one has a long hoot. I'm afraid it has a broken wing and it had to have its wing off, poor old thing. They all kill with their feet, of course, and that's why the talons are so big. They don't kill with their bills. They jump on an animal and kill it with their talons and then just tear it to pieces.'

Next is the beautiful barn owl with its white face and staring black eyes, which have been the cause of many a country ghost story. 'This one is my favourite. It's been associated with man for ever. A most lovely bird. There's been a terrible decline in its numbers in the last 10 or 15 years. It's apparently not due to pesticides. More to do with the loss of habitat with all the old Kent barns going and being replaced by metal Dutch barns. They just seem to have lost their homes and they've become quite rare, so I breed quite a lot of barn owls and release them into the wild.'

In a separate shed a huge eagle owl is looking at his smaller brothers and sisters with some contempt. This is one of the biggest owls in the world. It comes from the Russian Steppes and from across the countries of Northern Europe. It would be very rare for a wild eagle owl to visit Britain. 'This magnificent and dangerous creature must have been imported under licence. It escaped from captivity and it was dragging a four foot rope and an iron ring behind it when it was caught. It's in beautiful condition and a very proud fellow indeed.'

There are not many people who have the knowledge and patience to care for wild creatures in the way that Alan Gardiner looks after his owls. Men like him are in the front line of defence against the dangers of modern life which confront the whole of the animal kingdom.

ANOTHER owl enthusiast is Dr. Jim Flegg, whose work is at the East Malling Research Institute, where they discover and invent new ways with fruit trees to help Kent's farmers. Jim is also an expert naturalist and an authority on the birds of the south-east. He often goes to admire the water life at Leeds Castle – just down the road from his home. Leeds is described, with some justification, as the most beautiful castle in Britain and, since it is surrounded by water, it is a haven for geese and water fowl.

'This is a perfect place for the birds. I think it's as simple as that. They've got woodland here. They've got the lake. They've got the fields. They've got just about everything going for them. It's got to be good feeding. It's got to be good living and that's why they're here. And, in many ways, you can appreciate why they enjoy it. It's marvellous scenery, because it's so mixed, and man made it mixed. And that's fascinating too. The Castle was put here by man. Kent is one of the driest counties in

Britain. Yet, because of man, there are streams and the moat of the Castle – all man-made. The birds seize on that opportunity, and in they come. They're not all native birds. There are also ornamental water fowl which are superb to look at. Sometimes they're much more colourful than our own birds. Then there's the backdrop of the Castle always there and then, in amongst that, there are our own birds like the mallard, lovely to watch and, if you get close to them, just as beautiful as some of the foreign birds. So what more could anyone want?'

Jim Flegg is one of those dedicated people who are willing to put up with great discomfort and to exercise much patience in their search for birds to watch and admire. Cold, wet, wind or heat do not deter them. But at Leeds Castle there is the rare luxury of being able to observe wild-life easily and in relative comfort. 'The birds here are used to people. You can see them and compare them with their overseas relatives, which is also great fun. For example, you can concentrate on the Canada Geese. Charles I was responsible for bringing them into this country. Obviously somebody had to discover North America before they could bring Canada Geese here. So then they were brought in as ornamental water fowl, and now we regard them as part of our own heritage. But where else can you see them at such close range?'

Leeds Castle is one of those increasingly rare places, which offer hope to those who fear that man is busily destroying all that is best and most beautiful in his environment. It is an irony that mighty battlements and fortifications are now playing a role in protecting wild birds from the destructive effects of human progress.

WHITE flannel, green grass, the click of bat on ball and the shade of ancient oaks are as likely to mean stool-ball as cricket on the borders of Kent and Sussex. It is reputed to be an even older game than the sport of Lords. It is played with much skill and elegance by teams of ladies from the Garden of England. It was not always so. In 1630 it was recorded that 'Maidstone was formerly a very profane town when stool-ball and other games were practised on the Lord's Day.' Chris Litchfield is Captain of the Groombridge team.

'The name was taken from the milkmaids playing the game. They used three-legged stools and, from what we can make out, they bowled with anything they could find – apples, stones, old wooden balls. Two or three girls played, hit the ball with the stool and ran. The way they got each other out then was by throwing the ball at the person that was running, because there were no wickets – just marks on the ground. Of course now we've made it a much more modern game with wickets to throw at instead of people.'

It is a competitive contest. The women, dressed as for tennis, hit the ball with venom, and the fielders hold hard catches, which draw applause from the spectators. 'The bat is made in the same sort of way as a cricket bat. It's made of willow and has a flat front and you really do need to strike the ball right in the middle. I don't bat a lot, but we've got plenty of good batsmen. I'm the wicket-keeper and I get lots of exercise back there, particularly if I miss one or two and have to chase after them. You certainly need to be fit to play well. They say that, during the War, men played the game as a form of recuperation. I'm not sure about that. I think they might have found it a bit too much like hard work.'

The attractive game continues into the autumn evening and, with a little imagination, it is possible to picture the Groombridge girls of the sixteenth and seventeenth centuries playing the same game in the same spot with equal enthusiasm. The clothes and the accents would be different, but the spirit would be the same.

THE Crowborough Ploughing Match and Show takes place on the first Wednesday in October. From all over the Garden of England men and women come to Crowborough to show off their skills, their crafts and their wares. There is heavy horse ploughing as well as tractor ploughing. There is a competition for gun dogs and for pets. And, of course, there is a marquee filled to overflowing with flowers, hops, vegetables and home-made wine and food. The show is held on Hamsell Wood Farm, near Eridge, the home of Chairman, John Capsey.

'Everything is going for you round here. It's one of the best parts of the whole world. The views alone make it all worthwhile. I've been ploughing myself for forty-five years. In fact, I ploughed in the first of these competitions, and I ploughed again when it was in its twenty-fifth year. When it gets to fifty I plan to be doing it again. Of course, the machinery has changed, but the skill is the same. The judges are looking for a ploughman that has gone straight and has buried all the trash – the straw and stubble and such like. He also needs to have left a furrow which you can work down to sow your corn in. In other words, it's got to be neat, it's got to be tidy, it's got to be straight and, if you've got all those put together, you've got something which you can go out and sow tomorrow. And that's what they're looking for.'

Above the fields where the tractors move back and forth under the steady hands of the competitors, the great Shire horses, with a jingle of chains and a tossing of heads, sweat and strain as they move to and fro. The men behind these ploughs fling their weight to left and to right to counter the stones or heavy lumps of clay, which can throw the plough off course. 'When I first left school I used to work with horses. It's damned hard work compared to these tractors today, with a nice, quiet cab and a radio. Most of the machines that are made today make a good job of ploughing. If there's any error, it's usually up in the cab. The drivers are willing to accept that and that's why you have these competitions – to find out who can make the best job of it, because if it was just a question of going and buying a machine we could all do that.'

For a variety of reasons, the great characters seem to be disappearing from the farms and the villages. 'We don't have as many as we did. A few of them are up in the churchyard. But sometimes there's somebody else to take over from them. I remember the last time the Ploughing Match was on this farm in 1958. A local man called Roy came to organise the putting up of the big tent. And this year the man

Apple blossom is a typical Kentish bloom of the springtime. London has always provided a ready market for the apples grown in the Garden of England.

The Peregrine falcon's survival is under threat in the wild from pesticides and collectors. The birds are still found in coastal areas of Britain, like this one photographed near Folkestone.

who came to put up the tent, said to me, "It's a good job that Roy isn't still about, because he got all my men drunk and, in the end, they couldn't put the tent up until the day of the Show". It was touch and go that year.'

In another field close to a wood, groups of men and women wait with their labradors and retrievers to put the dogs through their paces. The gun is shot. But the dog must not move until given the command. There is a stile to jump and then the quarry — a small bag — to find and retrieve. 'The gun dogs come onto this farm four or five times a year. What the judges are looking for is a dog that will be very obedient indeed and that will go and pick up a bird and bring it back without running off somewhere else. Speed does come into it. But it's not the crucial thing. The vital factor is to bring the bird back and to take it to the right place without marking it. It's not much good bringing back a chewed up pheasant in record time.'

MANY people think that the only time to visit the Garden of England is in the spring, when the blossom is out. But the area is alive with beauty and warm with welcome throughout the year. Next time you sink your teeth into a Cox's Orange Pippin, or enjoy strawberries and cream to the sound of cricket, try to remember the Valley of the Owls and the fertile land that stretches around it. Remember too the men and women who work there throughout the year in fair weather and in foul to bring you the fruits of their labours. The Garden of England is certainly beautiful and productive but, like most gardens, it demands a mass of sweat and toil.

THE NORTH DOWNS

THE North Downs stretch from Guildford to the White Cliffs of Dover. Travellers on their way to the south coast and the Channel ports often speed past this unknown and beautiful part of the country unaware of its existence. The Downs were first settled six thousand years ago and since those days the high road over the Weald – better known as The Pilgrims' Way – has been walked by Romans and by Christians on pilgrimage to Canterbury Cathedral. Millions of years ago these hills – so much less well-known than the neighbouring South Downs – were part of the sea-bed, and the chalky soil gives the North Downs their particular character and quality. They include a wide variety of soft hills, dry river valleys and woodland, and they make gentle pasture for thousands of sheep.

Although much of the woodland has been cleared from the Downs, there is still a thriving industry from the copses and woods which remain. Uncounted fence posts are needed to contain cattle and sheep which have been grazed on these slopes since Neolithic times. And local oak has been widely used to build farm cottages, many of which have now become the homes of London commuters, who fall in love with the old beams. It is a curiosity of human nature that the Victorians often covered up the old timbers, because they thought that it turned them into peasants to live in such rough houses. Today, beams are all the fashion for those who can afford them.

The soil on the North Downs is often poor. The clay in the valleys is rough and flinty, though it is used effectively in local bricks and tiles. The flints themselves have been a valuable building material in churches, walls and houses, even if they have been a traditional enemy to anyone trying to cultivate the earth. Across the region today farmers have managed to plough the heavy land and, with modern equipment and fertilizers, they grow successful crops of wheat and barley.

ONE of the sad things about modern farms is that most of their fences are built of barbed-wire, and hedges are cut straight across by tractor-driven, circular saws. But Charles Hill from Petham near Canterbury is one of those rare people who can still lay hedges in the traditional way. His skill means that he constructs strong barriers and, at the same time, preserves wild-life.

'My father used to come to Kent for holidays every year in the 1930s, and he said that, if ever he changed his county, he would come to Kent. So I came down to Kent, and I've been here 37 years now. Laying hedges isn't very complicated really. People

The chalky soil gives the North Downs their particular character and ecology.

are afraid to do it somehow. They think it's such hard work. Of course it is hard work if you have very big trees in the hedges.'

Charles works swiftly and neatly. His sickle flashes in the spring sunshine as he cuts deep into the branches and then lays them on their sides to make a firm barricade of wood. 'You can cut nine-tenths of the way through three or four inch stems and leave what looks like just a little strap of bark. There'll still be plenty left. It'll never die while there's a bit of meat on it and a little bit of bark as well. It's absolutely proof against cattle or sheep.'

Watching him at work, it is hard to picture the new growth which will soon surge up through the hedge as a direct result of what he is doing. 'All the new stocks that I've cut will grow up from the bottom again, and all the pieces that are laid along on their sides will also shoot up and grow through the hedge to make a mass of greenery – a solid wall. And then once you've got your hedge laid nicely and looking trim you can use a modern implement, like a flail, to keep it tidy.'

In an ideal world, Charles Hill would do all his hedge-laying in the autumn and winter. 'From a vital, countryside point of view you should have finished doing this kind of work by mid-April – certainly no later – because of the birds building their nests and laying.' It is a gentle sight on a quiet Kent hillside as Charles works his way slowly and methodically along the growing hedge. It is a sight which must have been repeated thousands of times over the centuries.

HAWKS have hunted their prey on the North Downs since time immemorial. Today, much of the food for those that remain is provided on the verges of the motorways, courtesy of speeding drivers. At Stelling Minnis Emma Ford and her husband, Steve, are keeping alive the traditions of falconry, and ensuring that these proud creatures continue to exist on the North Downs. 'It is the oldest sport in the world. It originated in China in about 2,000 B.C. and, as civilisation spread westward, falconry moved with it.'

The rows of hawks are in magnificent condition as they sit proudly on their perches, hoping and waiting for action. 'One of my favourites is our male peregrine falcon. He's called a tiercel from the French word meaning a third because the males are a third smaller than the females. That's the case with all birds of prey that hunt in the daytime – the females are always that bit bigger than the males. Most of them are bred in captivity nowadays. We have our own breeding programme and the majority of falconers in the country now have started breeding their own birds.'

As the falcons soar and catch the wind, the tips of their wing feathers bend up towards the sky in their powerful flight. 'We fly for hunting in this area, which is rather enclosed. It's very wooded and hilly and you really need a short-winged bird – one of the buzzard family; a true hawk like a goshawk or a sparrowhawk. We tend to use species called Harris hawks, which come from Mexico. They're reliable. They've got a good instinct for quarry, and they're quick and manoeuvrable in this sort of countryside.'

At Stelling Minnis, Emma Ford and her husband Steve are keeping alive the traditions of falconry. As well as training peregrine falcons, they keep Harris hawks and a magnificent golden eagle.

One of the most important ways in which the Fords can keep falconry alive, is to teach enthusiasts the ancient skills and techniques. 'Beginners start with a common buzzard, which is a steady bird and can take a certain amount of rough handling. They also have some hunting potential, which is what falconry is all about. Generally speaking the buzzards train the people rather than the other way round. And they're a lovely sight when there's a bit of wind to give them buoyancy.'

The falcons need nearly as much training as their handlers. 'It would take about three weeks for the basic training of a bird and, with something like a Peregrine, you'd be looking at another couple of weeks to get it fit. It's one thing to train a bird of prey, but it's another to make it fit enough to take on quarry, which lives wild and free in its own habitat. What you're doing is pitting something that's been kept in captivity against that.'

The pride of Stelling Minnis is a magnificent golden eagle with ferocious talons and a mighty wingspan. 'We hunt him at rabbit and hare and we try to take him north each winter. You have to fly eagles mainly in the winter, because then there's normally enough wind to give them lift. So we take them up to the wide open spaces of Yorkshire or Scotland. I would prefer to live somewhere a bit more open than the North Downs, which would offer better grounds for hunting long-winged falcons. But I feel tremendously lucky to be able to do something as exhilarating as this full-time.' The great birds swing and weave in the wind currents above the downland and, as the lure circles and falls to the ground, they swoop into the attack.

THE North Downs are famous for the number and variety of plants and flowers which grow there. Thirty of the forty-seven British orchids have been found in the area. John Duffield used to work as Warden of the Wye Nature Reserve. He lives in a charming cottage beside a tumbling chalk stream at Brook near Ashford, and he

John Duffield is an expert on the wild flowers of the North Downs, an area famous for the number and variety of plants and flowers which grow there.

34

is an expert on the wild flowers of the Downs.

'Well, they've been my life, I suppose I can say, for sixty-five years. I was brought up on these hills and I think they must be in my bones. Chalk streams, like the one by my home, are not all that common in this part of the world. And the water has brought with it some of the most beautiful flowers on the silt that's been carried down over many years. There is so much reward in finding them for the people who will just take the time and trouble to look. For instance, something as common as the kingcup or marsh marigold is a magnificent sight. They always grow on the wetlands, and they seem to be equally happy whether it's chalk or acid soil. And that deep yellow colour is glorious beside the clear water. Of course, they're at the large end of the golden plants of spring. Just as beautiful is the little, golden saxifrage with its neat, tufted foliage. It grows happily in the same conditions as the kingcups.'

John Duffield goes for long walks across the Downs in search of flowers. The way the grassland is grazed and treated is vital if flowers are to have the chance to grow. A tremendous quantity have disappeared since the rabbits died out in 1953 — particularly the hairy violet, which used to be seen in blue masses on the hillsides. But there are still plenty of exquisite orchids, including the very first one to appear on the Downs. 'It's the early purple orchid, known round here as "skeetslegs". It's meant to have the scent of tom-cats. I remember when I was small I'd never be allowed to bring them into the house. My mother always said they smelled. But there's such a strong smell of thyme on the hillside that I can't usually sense anything unpleasant. Anyway, the colour is beautiful and so is the shape and, when they grow up, they can be as tall as twelve inches. I don't think there's much to choose between these and some of the rarer ones that such a fuss is made about.'

In the fold of the hills on a wild and uncultivated meadow is another rare sight which used to be a commonplace. Patches of bright, yellow cowslips are bending and nodding in the breeze. 'These are gorgeous. I think they are my favourite flowers. And they're marvellous examples up here — huge flowers with lots of florets on the heads. I think they've done well here, because we are at the foot of a slope and the soils are deeper. The further up you go, the smaller the flowers become. It's a beautiful and traditional English plant — at one time typical of most meadows. Now sadly it's confined to these hills because it's been impossible to plough here and it's not been worth putting down fertilizer or weed-killers.' Long may it be before it becomes worthwhile or possible to rip up and cultivate the steep sides of the North Downs. They are worth keeping just as they are for the sake of the cowslips alone.

PEOPLE in Kent claim that the taste of the best beer in the world is due to the quality of the hops which they have grown in the county over the centuries. Hop-gardens, with their unique lines of poles and wires making fascinating geometrical patterns, are a common sight on the North Downs. Hops are a delicate, time-consuming yet profitable enterprise. William Alexander and his family grow them with skill and success at Shoreham.

'I've been on this farm since 1951 when I got married. My father came down here from Scotland in 1892 and, as you know, they always export the best from Scotland. So I went back there in 1951 to get a wife. I have a parchment map in the farmhouse, which is dated 1720, and it shows hops growing in the same place then as they are now.'

The Alexanders' year starts as soon as the harvest is in in the autumn. They have to cut off any of the old vine that has been left over and renew any of the tall poles which have rotted through age and weather. The wire has to be made perfect. The poles and the wire work have a twenty year life. The poles are boiled in creosote to make them last and the wire is galvanised to give it a longer life. 'In the spring our first job is hop-stringing. It's done in March or April and the yarn is made with coconut fibre – the same as you get with coconut mats. We use twelve miles of yarn in every acre – an enormous amount. It only lasts one year and the reason for using this type of string is that, in the days when we picked by hand, the yarn would break and let the vine fall when the pickers pulled at it. This is still just as important with the modern machinery so that, when the vine is going through the machine, the string will break. We started machine-picking in 1960. When we were hand-picking we had eighteen acres and two hundred people picking by hand. Now we have twenty-eight acres and our complete staff is thirteen – that is in the hop-gardens, the picking machine and the drier. We start picking in September and it takes us three or four weeks to clear the lot.'

Once the hops begin to grow in the springtime, they have to be trained to climb the strings – each plant has its individual strings. 'It's a non-stop job for a number of women training the hops out in the hop gardens. In addition, we have to spray every ten to fourteen days against disease. It's a very delicate crop and easily affected by weather and disease. Once you've planted a new hop, it can last for ten, twenty, thirty or even forty years. We do change our variety from time to time, either because a better one has become available or because we may have had too much disease in a particular crop.'

William Alexander is justifiably proud of his produce and of the neat and meticulous farming, which he and his family have brought from Scotland to this special corner of Kent. 'The beer that's been produced from Kentish hops is the very best quality. You can be sure of that.'

THE North Downs are surrounded by motorways and railways. They are flown over by millions of holiday-makers on their way to the sun. For some reason this has only increased their isolation and remoteness. The distant roar of traffic is always with you, yet the scenery, the wildlife and the beauty remain untouched. Narrow lanes wind their way through bluebell woods and along lazy valleys. And the villages seem to turn a blind eye to the passing multitudes. It is as though, in spite of his best efforts, man has failed to destroy something precious, tranquil and quintessentially English. Perhaps, in the end, nature always does win.

ISLE OF SHEPPEY

THE Isle of Sheppey sits as a five by nine mile stopper in the mouth of the river Thames. There is nothing much except water and ice between Sheppey and the Arctic so when the north wind blows, it is a bitterly cold and bleak place. During the great east coast floods of 1953 Sheppey was cut off from the mainland. Access was only possible by boat from Rochester to Sheerness. But the marshy remoteness of the place makes it a sanctuary for waterfowl of every kind.

Sheppey is full of surprises. It was once a prime holiday resort for London's East Enders. Holiday chalets jostle beside magnificent churches and ancient inns. Agriculture and industry are close neighbours. Drive round a corner in the small town of Minster and, in a traditional English meadow full of chickens, ducks and ponies, you are faced by two llamas and a camel – sad relics of some abandoned circus and certainly an exceptional example of racial integration. By any standards Sheppey is an unpredictable place.

Sheppey means the Isle of Sheep. It was a special breed of sheep, now extinct, which grazed the salt marshes of the estuary and whose meat earned its flavour from the salt. The island was only joined to the mainland in relatively recent times, but to the inhabitants it remains an island. There are said to be people who have never crossed the water, and there is the in-bred feeling of a small and enclosed community. Locals are defensive about the place and quick to take offence if criticisms are aired. Like all historic, waterbound places there is a long tradition of smuggling and illicit dealings, and Sheppey has also played its part in the more open history of Britain.

Nelson lived on the island and kept his mistress, Lady Hamilton, at Queenborough. The painter, Hogarth, came and made sketches here. And Sir Roger Livesey, one of the judges who signed the death warrant of Charles I, owned the dockyard at Sheerness and lived nearby. At the time of Dunkirk in 1940, many of the little ships set out from Sheppey to rescue the British Army from the beaches of Northern France. And the rescued and the wounded were brought back to the island.

Perhaps the most dramatic change in the Isle of Sheppey's history came in 1960 with the closing of what had for centuries been a vast and thriving dockyard and Royal Navy garrison at Sheerness. The disappearance of the Navy from the island struck a blow to its morale and its economy from which it has yet to recover.

AGRICULTURE plays an important role in the life of the Isle of Sheppey. Cereals are taking over from sheep and cattle, except on the marshlands, where only grass will grow. Marion Studd farms the high land at Eastchurch. She is as pure Sheppey as you can find, coming from a line of farmers which goes back several generations in the area. She speaks with a soft, rural burr and is a loyal and enthusiastic islanders. 'My great grandparents and grandparents were born here and came to this farm in 1876. My father was a great stockman and I seem to have inherited his love of animals. I certainly prefer the livestock to the arable side.'

Her house is simple but solid, untidy and hospitable. The farmyard is a working place without frills and the flat land stretches away on all sides. Marion, a strong, upright woman with a warm face calls her sheep-dog and heads off to look over her ewes. 'They're mostly Kent ewes. But we run three different types of ram – Suffolk, Kent and Hampshire. I am never lonely because I've got the animals around me, and they know as much as what human beings do. Although there's 136 sheep out there – give or take a few – there are still the characters that you know.'

Next job for Marion is to feed a yard of bullocks. As she collects the corn, a flock of noisy geese waddles up the drive and flops into the muddy, farm pond. The sheepdog starts trying to herd a bunch of ducks, which are not willing to follow the same rules as the ewes in the meadow. And a large and colourful cockerel stands on guard in a cleft in a brick wall and shrieks defiance at the world. 'Well, it's seven days a week work, and sometimes seven nights a week too when you're lambing and calving. You've just got to be there all the time then. It's always been that way and, as far as I'm concerned, it always will be. We do try and adopt modern methods, but you can't make an animal have six legs instead of four, because that's the way they've been made. I think working close to nature is a good life. There's always something going on. There's always something changing. And I think that, in the country, you get a closer feeling for life and reality. I don't know what the town people would think though.'

In the farm house the fire crackles in the grate as the wind and rain beat against the windows. Everything is peaceful and warm as Marion gets down to her evening's work spinning wool. On a shelf is a box of corn dollies which she has made from wheat straw during the summer. 'I do quite a bit of craft work in between the farming. For the last year or so I've been nicking the fleece of the old, black sheep because you don't have to dye it. There's a natural shade in it. Sheppey is a way of life for me. It's where I've always been. This is what I've always done. I can't see myself fitting in anywhere else.' And her head bends down to her work again, and the old dog sleeps peacefully by the fire.

ELMLEY bird sanctuary is a by-word for water-fowlers from all over Britain and Europe. It is a huge marsh to the south of the island, grazed by slow, red cattle and sturdy sheep, and populated by thousands of geese and ducks. If you were dropped there by parachute, you might imagine that you had landed in the

When the day's farm work is done, Marion Studd relaxes by carding and spinning wool from her own sheep on her farm at Eastchurch.

Australian outback or the Canadian wilderness. Les Street is the Warden at Elmley and is responsible for the well-being of cattle, sheep and birds.

'My home at Kingsfield Farm must be one of the most remote places in south-east England. Although it might be a bit inhospitable for some folk, and although the open flats and windswept marshes may not perhaps be everybody's cup of tea, there's something about it that I really enjoy.'

Clad in green waterproofs, Les strides along the sea-walls and watches the kestrels and the short-eared owls hunting in the tussocks of coarse grass. 'I've been a keen bird-watcher for most of my life and I've always been interested in every kind of wild creature. As a teenager I used to bird-watch here on the Sheppey Marshes and on all the north Kent shore-line. This whole area of grassland, not only Spitend Marsh and Elmley Marsh, but the whole surrounding area forms one of the largest pieces of unploughed and undeveloped marshland in the country, and certainly in southern England. Consequently it's got a large wildlife population. The use of herbicides and insecticides is almost non-existent and the drainage is still fairly poor, leaving lots of fleets and ditches, which fill up in winter time. And it's these that are particularly important for the large numbers of wetland birds that use the area. Most of the birds are wigeon. They breed in Siberia and they spend the winter with us. We get something like twenty thousand of them returning here in the winter. It really is quite an important site for them.'

Elmley can feel a bit like Siberia during the winter months. When time presses, Les Street rides his range on a battered motorbike and two faithful sheep-dogs as pillion passengers. They sit firmly on the petrol tank and the rear saddle as the bike lurches over the rough terrain. 'It can be cold, though a lot of the birds come here to escape the Siberian winter. So they find it reasonably mild. The colder the weather becomes the more attractive it is for watching wild-fowl. The wind is the least comfortable part of the weather in winter on the marshes. There are no trees or anything to stop it once it starts blowing. Quite often you find yourself walking along at a 45 degree angle to avoid falling over.'

The cattle and sheep need constant attention at all times of the year and this makes heavy and time-consuming work for Les. 'A lot of the job involves looking after upwards of three hundred cattle throughout the summer. This drops right down to just a handful during the winter time. Only the biggest and hardiest ones are left out to brave the elements of Sheppey during the cold months. What we try to do is to manage the nature reserve with the livestock, in order to provide a mosaic of different habitats – long grass, medium grass with little tussocks to nest in, and short bowling greens for the wigeons and the geese to feed on. The sea-walls are not grazed, because we obviously don't want the animals to roam off into the mud flats and salt marshes and to get drowned. As a result there are more little mammals, like short-tailed voles and mice in the very long grass that is on the sea-walls. This rank grass is a haven for the rodents and, as a result, a perfect hunting ground for owls and hawks.' As the sun sets in a hundred colours of red and gold and crimson and the water reflects the splendour of the evening, a small fishing-boat chugs out to sea and flocks of geese and ducks fly neatly in for their night's rest.

IT is impossible to visit the Isle of Sheppey without being aware of the dockyard at Sheerness, where so much of the Island's history has been written. Nobody could claim that Sheerness is a beauty spot. Once a massive naval base it is now a bustling, industrial port, and the new, Japanese cars being driven in their thousands at break-neck speeds off the transport ships explain the looks of astonishment on the faces of the old sailing-ship figureheads which decorate and grace the area. Veteran Bert Shardlow has worked in the dockyard for most of his life and remembers some of the old days well. 'I first came to the Isle of Sheppey with Sunday School outings from Stroud, up near Rochester. We arrived at Sheerness Pier and we had a long walk around the dockyard wall and eventually went up to the sea front where, it seemed to me, it was always raining.'

Bert is strong, straight and upright for a man of his years, and regrets the passing of the dockyard's great days. 'When I first came to work here in 1939 we were only undertaking the refits of very small warships. It brings back a lot of memories seeing the docks as they are today. Memories of going out from here of a night, refitting ships out in the stream, out beyond the boom. Dirty, heavy work. And I remember the small boats going off to France and coming back. They came here from all over the place and included local ones. The dockyard tugs themselves set out for Dunkirk from here. And, although they never all returned here with survivors, some of them did. As far as the dockyard itself is concerned, it was always short of facilities – badly equipped, but the craftsmen were good. We all learnt to be inventive and innovative to make up for the poor equipment.'

Bert Shardlow is one of a dying breed. They do not seem to build them like that anymore. And, although technology can replace and probably surpass his skills, it cannot even start to make up for the strength of character and determination which are vanishing forever.

ANGELA Walder's life is spent rescuing and protecting animals from the harm often inflicted upon them by man. Her home, on the outskirts of Minster, is aptly named Arcadia and is full of creatures which she has saved. 'There's my cat, which came from the East End animal market. We found it in a cardboard box one Sunday. It had just been thrown out for the Council tip van, and it was a frightened little creature. But now she runs about enjoying life.'

Angela is dedicated to her animals and spends much of her time at home caring for them, feeding them and strolling among them. As she walks down her little paddock she is surrounded by chickens, geese, cats and goats. 'The white goat is blind, I'm afraid. She'd been blinded in a laboratory and we got her when she was still quite young. She's now nearly ten years old. We brought her here and put her in this little meadow, where we don't move anything, so that she can find her way around. I

The Isle of Sheppey is an isolated area of Britain, a place of peace and solitude.

think she can probably see shadows. In the end I got another goat for her as a companion, and they just wander around here. But it's sad that she can't enjoy as much of the countryside as she should be able to.'

Although there are houses and roads nearby, Angela has managed to create a small haven on her land. Close to her house is an aviary full of attractive birds, including a fine, green and yellow parrot, which came from a pet shop in London. 'He was practically featherless when we found him there. He was obviously very sick. So we kept him in a cage for a little while and looked after him until he got better. And now he's out in the aviary in beautiful condition.

'For me, Sheppey is an escape from the concrete jungle of London. Just somewhere I can come to where there is peace and quiet, and where I can roam about undisturbed. It's the simplicity of it that I like most.'

THE Isle of Sheppey is a place of peace and isolation. Some of the island's communities, like Shellness, do not welcome strangers, in case the dreaded outsiders find out about it and invade its solitude. On the other hand, there is the urban sprawl at Laysdown and the socially-deprived area of Sheerness which, by universal agreement, have been brought about by uncontrolled development decisions. All the same, there is still a mass of genuine and unique countryside and wildlife on the island, and the haunting sounds of the geese and ducks at dawn and dusk are a constant reminder of the special qualities of this almost unknown part of Britain.

ISLE OF THANET

THE Isle of Thanet points like a stubby, accusing finger into the North Sea from the top, right-hand corner of Kent. There is little to protect Thanet from the winds which blow from the frozen North. So it can be a bitterly cold and inhospitable area. Ironically though, it contains some of the South's premier holiday resorts: Ramsgate, Margate and Broadstairs. And in the heat of summer there is no more pleasant place to be beside the sea. In the winter months it is bleak and bitter. But there is still plenty to see and to experience as animals, plants and humans hope for the first touches of spring. A mediaeval monk's description of the Isle of Thanet reads: 'Thanet, round Isle, by water compassed, reckoned Fertile and clean, to none on earth the second.'

And the waves which pound the island's shore are the ones which brought Hengist and Horsa from Jutland to this country 1500 years ago when, according to the historian J. R. Green, 'English history begins'. Traces of the area's antiquity remain to this day, though much has vanished beneath the urban sprawl and the rich fields of vegetables. It would be hard for even the most loyal inhabitant of Thanet to describe the area as a beauty spot, but there remain pockets of real splendour and places along the coast which are relatively unspoilt.

Probably Thanet's most famous visitor was Charles Dickens. He first came to Broadstairs in 1837 and called it 'our little watering place'. He returned again and again for holidays and to write. Bleak House, which overlooks the Channel from the cliffs, was called Fort House when he stayed there to complete David Copperfield. And it seems likely that he was inspired to write his famous novel *Bleak House* by the gaunt building on the cliffs.

THERE has been a lighthouse on Thanet's North Foreland since 1505, when it would have been lit by candles. Local historians claim that, when the tower burned down in 1683, a glass lantern on a pole was used to warn shipping. A new lighthouse was built in 1693 and, in 1790, the height of the tower was increased to nearly sixty-five feet. The notorious Goodwin Sands — perhaps the most treacherous shallows in the English Channel — lie close off-shore. And keeper Jim Bowling, who has been in the service for over forty years, has to be constantly on the alert. But there are some consolations at the North Foreland lighthouse compared to the longships off Lands End, where Jim started work.

The lighthouse at Thanet's North Foreland has been warning shipping since 1505. Then it was lit by candles; today computers and electronics reign. Even so, keeper Jim Bowling still has to climb to the top of the tower to polish the glass lenses round the great light.

'One of the pleasant things about a shore station is that you can have your family living with you. You've got married quarters and you can almost lead a normal, family life. On the lighthouse out at sea, like the Wolf Rock, the three keepers are there on their own and the wives and families stay on shore.'

At first glance the inside of the North Foreland Lighthouse is just as you would expect it to be. It is a tall tube of a building, painted yellow, with a steep staircase winding its way up towards the light at the top. The walls are thick and there are

The grey squirrel – a bold little animal equally at home in town gardens and country woodland.

Off Thanet's North Foreland lies 'The Great Ship Swallower' – the notorious Goodwin Sands on which so many ships have been wrecked.

occasional slit windows letting in some daylight. But, at ground level, modern technology has arrived and, with the chattering of print-outs and the flickering of screens, it looks more like a cross between a telephone exchange and a space station than a lighthouse. 'I'm afraid the computer is taking over here, as it is everywhere else. And there's no denying that it's a clever piece of equipment, because we are eventually going to control nine stations from here.'

It is not all electronics though. Armed only with a duster and the strength of his arm, Jim regularly climbs to the top of the tower to shine and polish the glass lenses round the great light. The prisms reflect all the colours of the rainbow. 'When the lower half of the tower was built nearly three hundred years ago, it was just a beacon and they burnt a fire on top of it. Then, much later, it was heightened and the top piece was put on in 1890. It was an oil light in those days. It was finally electrified in 1930 and the 3000 watts gives us a range of twenty miles.'

On the balcony outside the light it is blowing a gale. The cold is numbing but the views out to sea are spectacular as the white water crashes onto the beach. 'The light itself is built up by the lens to 175,000 candle-power. It's all been focused out to sea, so you don't get the effect of it when you're close up to it. Days gone by they used to get an awful lot of wrecks on the Goodwin Sands. This lighthouse was originally built specially to mark them. But then, with the advent of the lightships, they put three of them around the Sands and then they raised this one to give it more range.'

Seen from the shore the trim, white tower stands comfortably above the skyline. As dusk falls the huge light begins to flash out its warning to the ships at sea, as it has done, in one form or another, over the centuries.

SOME people say that greyhound racing is a dying sport. It is supposed to lack the glamour of horse-racing, the violence of football and the class of cricket. But you would never believe that it was on the wane if you visited greyhound trainer Peter Rich's bustling kennels just across the road from Thanet's smart racing track, Dumpton Park, at Ramsgate.

'I came down here from the London area. The pace is a lot slower down here and it suits me. The dogs – they're all made different. They're either sprinters or stayers. You can't make a sprinter stay and you can't make a stayer sprint. Most of the dogs I've got have been schooled before they come to me. It's a natural thing. They're bred to chase. They would chase anything. There have been occasions when the traps have opened before the hare's got there and the dogs have still gone racing round the track. They just love to race.'

At one end of the kennels are the young dogs, affectionate and full of fun. At regular intervals men and women walk briskly back from the nearby parks with strings of five or six greyhounds, which they have been exercising. Inside, a vast lunch of minced meat and vegetables is being prepared in an old enamel bath-tub. Greyhounds are being weighed, having their toe-nails clipped, being groomed, having their teeth brushed and being treated with ultrasonics for strains and bruises.

It is a predictably busy and animated scene, marred only by the pervading smell of the steaming food and the scores of dogs kept together at close quarters. 'They can start racing at fifteen months old, and some dogs run through till they're five or five and a half. It depends how lucky they are with injuries, because they can shorten their careers. Not too many of them go to stud, because they've got to be really outstanding to be able to make it there. One of our problems is finding good homes for 'em when they do retire. You might not think it, but they make lovely pets. Sometimes people don't believe it, but you can retrain them to be domestic animals and they're really great, once they've settled down a bit.'

Out on the frozen sands at Pegwell Bay, Peter Rich sometimes takes his stream-lined sprinters for practise runs on a winter's afternoon. He has to wait until anyone out for a bracing walk with his pet dog has vanished into the distance, in case the greyhounds mistake the pet for a hare. Once released the dogs fly across the grey sand and the spray from their rushing feet flashes and sparkles in the misty sunshine.

THE harsh winter weather, combined with the oil jettisoned by passing tankers, kills thousands of lovely sea-birds each year. It is a common sight to see a gull or a guillemot struggling in the foam as the waves wash in, unable to fly or to swim against the current. Hundreds of these frozen creatures are rescued and saved by Ian Hunter and his dedicated team at the Sandwich Bay Bird Observatory.

'This is a bit unusual as an observatory, because most of them seem to be on peninsulas or islands. But, being on the south coast and very near the Continent helps us to get quite a variety of migrating birds. This is a good place for the land-fall for small migrants particularly and there's some fine, coastal bird-watching. And we're also very lucky in having an estuary nearby, so we get a good selection of waders – just the common stuff like curlews and oyster-catchers, but last spring we had a broad-billed sandpiper, just to add a bit of spice to life.'

Ian and his team were well-clothed against the cold in what was one of the coldest February weeks for decades on the Isle of Thanet. Never once did the temperature break through the freezing barrier and they learnt all about chill factors. The thermometer sometimes sank to −15 degrees centigrade and gale force north-easterly winds straight from Siberia whipped up the seas. 'The birds are really suffering. The shore is freezing up a lot, so it's difficult for them. If it stays frozen they'll soon start dispersing, trying to find less icy places.'

In the grass meadow behind the ramshackle Observatory buildings birds are netted and ringed. Usually the captives are nothing more special than starlings or sparrows, but sometimes there is the excitement of a snipe with its long, pointed bill and quick-silver flight. All are treated gently and with great care. 'We catch them out in the fields and we immediately put the birds in cotton bags. This stops damage to the plumage because they don't panic in there. It's dark, so they don't see sharp movements and it settles them down. We bring them back indoors and put an individually-numbered ring on them with a return address on it. Then, if anyone finds the bird in a field, they can get the information back to us via the British Trust for Ornithology. We also age and sex the birds, using methods that have been built up over the years, and we weigh them and measure their wings – just taking the information that will help us to understand how the population is doing.'

The snipe is passed gently along the line and the details are noted. The long bill sticks out of the bag like a grey knitting-needle. It receives ring number 50 and is released and held on a gloved hand out of the window. It hesitates for a few seconds, regretting the comparative warmth, and then darts away in a twisting blur towards the snow-covered meadows. 'Particularly at this time of year and in this kind of weather we keep a very close eye on their weights and how they're doing. Obviously, they do suffer and so we have to start thinking about putting out more food and also we may have to stop ringing. Because we don't want to distress the birds at all when they're already having a bad time.'

Later in the day a large red, green, gold and brown bird is netted. It puts up a furious struggle before submitting to the outrage. From a distance it looks far too glamorous to be an English bird. The colours would look in place in the south Pacific. But, in fact, it is a green woodpecker. 'It's quite clear, apart from the red, why it is called a green woodpecker. We've been able to age and sex it. It's got a black moustache stripe, which makes it a female. The male's would be red. And there are various characteristics on the feathers, which have helped us to age it.'

The bird uses its formidable beak to peck furiously at the hands that are holding it. Its claws are also trying hard to lay hold of any finger that offers itself. 'It hangs onto tree-trunks with those sharp claws. That's why I handle it round the angles, so it doesn't get hold of me. The other interesting thing is its very stiff tail. The feathers are still to help prop it up if it wants to climb up a tree – a bit like a built-in shooting stick. And, of course, the gold on his front is really magnificent. But, in this weather, I think it's time it went back out to get a bit of feeding in. It's very important that we don't hang onto the birds too long. So I'll point him out into the open fields and he'll head on to the trees beyond – if only he'll let go of my fingers.' In a glow of many colours the woodpecker flies off into the distance in search of something, which will yield more satisfaction than a human hand.

MUCH of Minster Abbey dates back to the Saxons. It was one of the first monasteries in England and was established by Domneva, who became the first abbess in 669 A.D. She was given the land by her uncle, King Egbert, to try to make up for the killing of her two brothers by the Saxon thane called Thunor. There is a story that the abbess was promised the amount of land, which could be covered in a single run by her tame deer. Thunor tried to get in the way of the deer and was drowned when he and his horse fell into a ditch. Less dramatically nowadays, the nuns spend their time at prayer and at work on their busy, twenty acre farm. In the chill candle-light of the small, Norman chapel, their breath steams as they sing their morning prayers. Out in the fields Sister Ancilla is hard at work cutting and carting kale for the livestock. 'We don't go in for a lot of concentrates for fertilizers. It's all organic. As far as people go, there are comings and goings. There's four of us who work the farm at intervals during the day. Then we've got a man who does fifteen hours a week. And, in the summer for haymaking, there are students who come and work for their keep, making hay and that sort of thing.'

It is a mediaeval sight as the nuns, in their working habits, move around the farmyard feeding and looking after the animals. In the background Minster Abbey stands unchanging through the centuries. 'We're more or less self-sufficient as far as feeding the stock is concerned. We just buy in Brewers' Grain instead of concentrates. It's a very good form of protein – particularly in a winter like this, when it has really been very cold. And the animals always do very well on it. There's something in it that isn't definable, and they just flourish on it.'

In one of the old, semi-covered yards a flock of well-fed sheep is getting its daily ration of hay and kale. They are quite recent arrivals at the Abbey farm. 'We're just beginning to recognise the individual sheep. They're not quite so easy to know as cows. When we first had them we thought we'd never distinguish one from the other. But they are very individual. We'll sell the fat lambs to Canterbury slaughter-house. And that should, more or less, pay for the overheads of the farm. We have to have some income coming in. Otherwise we wouldn't be viable. And the steers will also be sold for slaughter when they're fully grown – that's at about fourteen months.'

The Mother Prioress at Minster Abbey is Sister Concordia. She is as bright as a button and speaks with affection about her life and work. She has one of those faces which shine with enthusiasm as she talks. In addition to her time-consuming religious duties, she is a skilled sculptress and has one of her many works in a position of honour in Canterbury Cathedral. Her studio is in a draughty stable built onto the Abbey wall. The stalls and the cobbled floor are unchanged since the days of the horses, and the Mother Prioress's works of art stand where the grooms once worked. 'Since I was six I always wanted to be nothing else but an artist. But my family didn't have any money, so I sat for a scholarship and, when I was 17, I got into the Edinburgh College of Art. Then, on my nineteenth birthday – it was the tail-end of the War – I was called up. So I was in the A.T.S. for three years. The war changed people a lot. It changed me a great deal. And I started to look around, and I heard about this place. So I came down to have a look at it. And I thought that if I was going to be a nun anywhere it would be here. And it was.'

There is a great peace in the Abbey and justifiable pride in living in and caring for a building so deeply touched by history. 'It's reckoned to be one of the oldest lived-in houses in England. The little Norman chapel, where we sometimes pray, goes back to 1027 – about forty years before the Conquest. But the very first monastery was founded in 670 A.D. It was built by the grand-daughter of the first Christian King of Kent. Thanet was a real island then. Where the railway station is now was the harbour, and it was a thriving community for about two hundred years. Then the Vikings sailed up and burnt it to the ground in the ninth century. There were about seventy nuns here then, and all the village people had run into the monastery for safety. Nobody survived.'

Long icicles hang like daggers from the gutters outside the old stables, and the windows are steamed up on the inside as the Mother Prioress works about at her latest figure. 'I think it's been the hardest winter I can remember, as far as the frost is concerned. I've never had any of my models frozen before. But, for nearly a fortnight, I haven't been able to work in here. It's been ice-hard. And today I thought I'd try and thaw him out – he's Saint Jude, patron of desperate causes. So I put on the electric blower and I think the surface of the clay must have started to flow with water, and it all cracked open and the hand fell off. So I've had to try to patch him up.'

THE village of St. Nicholas-at-Wade is said to get its name from the days when, centuries ago, it first became possible to wade from the Island of Thanet to the Kent mainland. Today the village is surrounded by fertile fields of prime vegetables, corn and potatoes – typical of the area and readily packed and shipped to London by hard-working, local farmers. Bread from the Oak Bakery at St. Nicholas-at-Wade was registered in the Guinness Book of Records when the baker, Ken Lambert, together with farming brothers Richard and Martin Tapp from St. Nicholas Mill in the village, managed to produce a finished loaf from standing corn in just fifty-two minutes. In their shining, new mill the Tapp brothers are producing up to ten tons of stoneground, wholewheat flour every week. Elsewhere on the farm, potatoes and vegetables are neatly packaged for delivery to some of the best-known shops in the country.

'This land offers a wonderfully wide range of vegetable cropping. The cold wind that you get off the sea at the moment lets us run early, unseasonal crops to some extent – like early potatoes. We get a good, cold drying wind in the early spring and we put the potatoes in and they don't get frosted. So we have an early crop round about the end of May. And certainly the mill has been a good boost to us with the increasing demand for food with fibre. Basically, the outer husk of the grain and the wheatgerm are retained after milling. Hence the darker colour of the flour and the high fibre content. 100% wholewheat flour contains all the fibre and germ of the whole grain. When the flour is stoneground instead of being rolled it has the added advantage of not being subjected to high temperatures, which destroy the natural oils and vitamins in the wheat.'

AS on many islands or former islands dotted around the British coast, Thanet's people are islanders through and through. In spite of busy roads, some awful architecture, Manston Airport and seaside caravans, there is still a wealth of history to savour and enjoy. If you love the sea you will find it in all its moods along the whole length of this, the Bulwark Shore.

THE PILGRIMS' WAY

THE Pilgrims' Way stretches from Southampton to Canterbury. There was almost certainly a track along its route in pre-Roman times. This was the road used by tin-merchants to transport their precious ingots from Cornwall to the ships at Sandwich Haven in Kent.

In July 1175 Henry II landed at Southampton from France and made his first pilgrimage to the tomb of Thomas-a-Becket, whose murder he had instigated. And it is this track, trodden by thousands of pilgrims over the next three centuries, which can still be clearly seen today along much of its course through Hampshire, Surrey and Kent.

The days of pilgrimages are over. But the road they trod still bears the name The Pilgrims' Way. Julia Cartwright described it in 1911. 'Over the Surrey hills and through her stately parks the dark yews, which lined the path, may yet be seen. By many a quiet, Kentish homestead the grassy track still winds its way along the lonely hillside overlooking the blue Weald and, if you ask its name, the labourer who guides the plough, or the waggoner driving his team, will tell you that it is the pilgrims' road to Canterbury. So the old name lives, and the memory of that famous pilgrimage, which Chaucer sang, has not yet died out of the people's heart. And, although strangers journey no longer from afar to the martyr's shrine, it is still a pleasant thing to ride out on a spring or summer morning and follow the Pilgrims' Way. For the scenes through which it leads are fair, and the memories that it wakes belong to the noblest pages of England's story.'

TODAY'S pilgrims go by motorway to Canterbury and the Channel ports. As their tyres scream along the new roads, they are blind and deaf to the history that surrounds them. All the romance has gone amidst the noise and the stress of modern travel. But the heavy-duty gravel, which is such a vital part of road-building, yields some benefits. Without its removal, the Sevenoaks Wildfowl Reserve would not exist under the gentle eye of its warden, John Tyler, who is also something of a thatcher. High up a ladder beside his home, which stands close to the lakes, John is carefully constructing a strong, reed roof for an outhouse. All around him are trees and water and greenery and birds. But the sound of traffic is a constant reminder of less pleasant things.

52

'This whole project was started about twenty years ago by the Harrison family. They took on what was then just a derelict gravel site – a string of pits with virtually no trees or plants. All the trees here have been planted in the last twenty years. It comes home to you, especially at night when you can see all the street lights through the trees, and you realise that you're totally surrounded by houses and factories. To mask out the buildings, something like thirteen thousand trees have been planted by hand.'

The lakes are heavily populated with water birds and fish. Geese and ducks, swans, coots, moorhens and herons go importantly about their business. The thick undergrowth provides perfect cover for song-birds and butterflies and a score of other insects. All appear to be at peace with the man-made hubbub, which drives in at them from every side. 'They seem totally to ignore the fact that they are living in the suburbs. We've had birds nesting in the lorries and on the sides of the lorry ramps, and they pay no attention to all the commotion. Because, although the pits here aren't worked any more, a lot of gravel still comes in on the train and there's a lot of moving and unloading of gravel. So there's still enormous numbers of lorries coming in and out all the time. And the birds are used to them, and seem quite happy.'

Narrow trails wind through the trees and over the damp ground, where logs have been laid to make access possible to the neat wooden hides which stand at vantage points beside the water. Through the narrow look-out slits you can have as near as possible a perfect view of a whole range of waterfowl and wild-life. 'We get everybody here really, from dedicated, single-minded bird watchers who come to see a particular species, down to people who just come to have a quiet walk. Sometimes we get artists and, of course, school groups to study nature. The main types of birds we get are ducks and geese over-wintering and lots of wading birds. They come in during the cold months and then they move off later on to breed elsewhere. We get things like Little Ring Plovers breeding here, but then they're a gravel pit speciality.'

As John is speaking a string of Canada geese lands noisily on the far side of the lake. Nearby a pike is clearly on the warpath because fish are leaping out of the water. One of them jumps straight up under a mallard which is swimming softly along minding its own business, and throws it off balance. The duck hurries off quacking in disgust at this unexpected attack from beneath. 'On the whole, all the different species get on reasonably well with each other, even though they're living at close quarters. You get minor fights, but generally they all benefit from the mix. The Canada Geese and the Swans tend to be a bit aggressive and to push the others out of the way. But nothing serious. And they're lucky really to be in such a unique place. It's the conquest of man over his environment – the fact that it is so natural but at the same time totally artificial. It's a created environment, but you couldn't tell it by looking at it.' And, binoculars at the ready, John Tyler disappears into his man-made jungle while the sound of a factory lunch-bell rings in the distance behind the trees.

The warden of the Sevenoaks Wildfowl Reserve, John Tyler. The Reserve was created from a derelict gravel site and is now home to all manner of water birds and fish.

ALTHOUGH much of the route of the Pilgrims' Way is still unspoilt countryside, that cannot be said of Snodland near Maidstone. In spite of the factory chimneys and the urban sprawl, the distant views of the North Downs along which the old trail runs are a permanent reminder of the tranquillity, which is close at hand. Within sight of the rolling hills and the eyesores of Snodland, self-taught carpenter Charlie Eldridge has borrowed a corner of his former employer's cement works to set up in business as a skilled and elegant craftsman in the old style. 'Last year I was made redundant so I decided that, as woodworking was a hobby in the past, I would try to take it up full-time. I haven't had any professional training but, once I'd started, I rather liked it. It's specially pleasing to try to make something with a bit of quality in it.'

The small workshop is in the back of a large warehouse. It is well-equipped and there are dangerous-looking electrical machines, as well as all the normal tools of a carpenter's trade. In one corner a perfect green and white doll's house is nearly finished. In another, a child's engine – red with a black smokestack – is waiting for its final coat of paint. Beneath the small window Charlie's son is hard at work on a baby's rocking-horse. And dominating everything is a large and beautiful traditional rocking-horse, which would stand with pride in the windows of Harrods or Selfridges. 'I try to make these rocking horses as close as possible in style and quality to the old Victorian type. I make the whole thing, right from the horse itself to fitting the bridle, the saddle, the adjustable stirrups, the stand, the swinger – everything. It takes me about three weeks to a month to make. But it's the smoothing down of the surface, painting it, waiting for it to dry and titivating it about that takes the time. I like to see a finished product that, if I was a customer, I would like to buy.'

Charlie and his son turn back to their work, hoping that there will be enough discerning customers to enable them to earn a decent living in the bracing world of the self-employed. If they are to be judged and rewarded by the quality of their work, they must come out on top.

IF Chaucer is anything to go by, much merry-making and ribaldry accompanied the Canterbury pilgrims on their long journey across the South of England. Although their pilgrimage had a serious and a religious purpose, they did not allow that to weigh too heavily upon them. Some echo of this attitude remains with the jaunty enthusiasm of the Wadard Morris Men and their Squire, Paul Stead. Outside the Chequers Inn at Heaverham they cheerfully hold up the traffic as they dance with tinkling bells and stamping feet on the Queen's highroad. As the pints of beer disappear the dancing becomes less precise but the atmosphere even more convivial. 'We draw our dancers from all over the area, from the Darent Valley and across to Dartford and into the country areas down as far as Wrotham. We dance at quite a lot of the pubs in the villages along the Pilgrims' Way. It's always on Wednesday evening in the summer, and we get a very good response from the people. I should think the pilgrims would have got the same sort of welcome.'

While the dancers move to and fro in line abreast, a small, slim man with spectacles prances about waving a jester's stick. He is dressed in colourful clothes and wears a top hat. He would not look out of place in a Christmas pantomime or in a Lord Mayor's procession of over fifty years ago. 'Every Morris team has a number of characters. We have a fool, who performs with the dancers. He has the hardest job of all really. He's there to entertain the crowd in between the dances.'

As the dancing continues children in the crowd run in and out among the dancers. A woman feeds a black lamb from a bottle, and dogs move uneasily, half-inclined to bark or growl. One of the Morris Men approaches the spectators menacingly with a drawn sword, and then offers them small pieces of almond cake, which are packed into the hilt. It is a popular move and the people surge around him. 'It originates a long way back. We're not sure where. Perhaps with the pilgrims. But a number of traditional teams have always had a sword, on which they could carry cake. It's meant to be a lucky, fertility cake – if you call that lucky – and it's given to the crowd as a kind of token.'

Paul is a big man – not a likely candidate for ballroom dancing or delicacy. But it is surprising how much finesse he and his friends manage to put into their performance. In addition, they do not look in the least effeminate in their strange, multi-coloured costumes. 'Our outfits are based on the colours of the village of Farningham, near Rochester. Our motif comes from the Bayeux tapestry. Sir Wadard, after whom we are called, came over with William the Conqueror. He gets a small piece of the Bayeux tapestry to himself, so that's where our emblem comes from. But the clothes don't matter too much. Once you're dancing you forget about everything else, and just concentrate on the steps and the movements.' And Paul and his friends dance merrily on to the delight of the customers at the pub and the frustration of the waiting motorists.

JUST to the south of the Pilgrims' Way stands Knole House, surrounded by ancient parkland. It is one of the great homes of England and stands serenely encircled by the beauty which has been created to set off its splendour. It was here that Vita Sackville-West spent her privileged and much-publicised childhood, before she went off to build her own fairyland at Sissinghurst. But it was to Knole that she always longed to return. The busy game-keeper there today is Ray West. 'I came from Devon originally. I gradually worked my way up through Hampshire and Wiltshire to Kent. And it's a very good place to be now I've got here and seeing it's so close to London. You just walk out of the main gate and you're in Sevenoaks itself. So, although it may feel like it, you're not really out in the wilds.'

Ray is every inch a game-keeper. His face is tanned. His eye is sharp, and his clothes are the colour of the countryside. He is genuinely fond of animals and his feelings about people are unmixed. 'I don't like them at all. They come and visit this parkland sometimes and we're pleased to see them, but we expect them to abide by the rules. I'm afraid you get some that step out of line and think rules are made for everybody else but them. That means that my job is twenty-four hours a day and three hundred and sixty-five days a year. I start in my own time – sometimes I'm up early and sometimes I'm up late – but I'm very seldom in bed before 1.30 in the morning. I'm lucky. I'm not told what to do. I do what I think has got to be done in the Park – controlling vermin and looking after the deer.'

The deer are everywhere. Large herds of fallow deer with their white summer spots graze between the mighty oaks and beeches. They are not wild, but they are not very tame either and they present Ray West with plenty of problems. 'We do get a bit

The deer are always much in evidence in the grounds of Knole House where Ray West the gamekeeper works long hours in all weathers to look after them.

of poaching, mostly in the winter. But we try to stamp down on it. It's more or less surveillance all the time. Deer can be very dangerous. We've got notices up warning of the danger, but visitors will still pick the fawns up. When they find a fawn, because it's not in a carry cot and its mother's not standing beside it, they think it's been abandoned. They pick it up and carry it round the Park for half a day, and then they come to me and say they've found it. And I ask them where they picked it up and they haven't got a clue. And then the doe won't take it back if it's got human scent on it. So those well-meaning people have signed the death warrant of that fawn.'

Ray moves slowly and silently through the bracken. The sun makes soft patterns through the green leaves and the trees are alive with birds and squirrels. In the distance deer move gently forward as they nibble the young grass. Ray stops and raises his arm and points. To the untutored eye there is still nothing, but he is standing within a couple of yards of a newborn, perfectly camouflaged fawn.

'It stays very still. It's got no scent for the first month of its life. And it can be quiet as death. If you stand over a newly-born one it will stop breathing for a minute and then, when it's forced to breathe, it will take very shallow breaths, so that you can hardly see the rise and fall. It's almost motionless. And with the spots it's so well

57

hidden that a lot of people can walk straight past them and they have no idea. The mother's milk is very thick. It's the consistency of custard. Very rich, so the fawn grows fast. And that's another part of their protection. They can soon run with their mothers – as fast as and soon, even faster than the does.'

High on a slope young bucks are scampering about and playing, while the old stags look on complacently without anxiety. The day will come when they may have more to fear. 'They've got to be a good five years old before they compete for the does. The young bucks try to move in then, but the old boys drive them out. You never get two bucks fight that aren't equally matched. But, when they are evenly matched, they will scrap for hours. And then, while the fight is going on, you'll sometimes get another buck creep in and steal a few of the does away while they're busy fighting.' Ray strides up the hill and away towards the fairy towers of Knole, and the deer move quietly aside as he walks amongst them.

ALL the old skills are dying out fast and hand-work is at a premium. At Otford, a group of ten women work together to produce the kind of patchwork quilts and cushions which no machine can make. The patterns are colourful and imaginative. The work is detailed and exact. Hands fly over the giant frame and the conversation flickers and dies and rekindles as concentration ebbs and flows. Founder of this talented team is Elizabeth Harris.

'This kind of work has been passed down over hundreds of years. We may be more comfortable now and warmer, and better dressed. But they've always had frames like this, even when they worked in tiny little cottages. Somehow they managed to have a frame in them. Long before the birth of Christ people were making such quilts. They've even seen examples of them in Egyptian carvings. I suppose it's understandable, because people have always needed to keep warm. A lot were made in the small village houses, and some very beautiful ones were made in Castles. So, to some extent, it was a classless occupation.'

Each of the women has one hand in action above the frame and one below, as the needles pass up and down through the fine material. Heads bend low and eyes focus on the pattern. It is vital that the end product looks as though it has been completed by one pair of hands and not by ten. Team work is important and the fine circular shapes slowly emerge and spread across the cloth. 'This is a wine-glass pattern which we copied from an old quilt. It's simply based on a circle, which you draw round, and then you move the circle and draw the next segments. It's a very simple pattern. Most of the best ones are. You could use a plate or a saucer instead of a wine-glass. It is one of many traditional patterns which you can always find a new way of using.'

As the rain lashes the window panes the steady work continues. Observed from outside it is a cosy and cheerful scene, and the work is creative and satisfying. 'It's an ideal occupation for a wet day. Or in the winter when it's cold and snowy. There's nothing better than all getting together round the quilting frame.'

Similar sights, with only the clothes and furniture and attitudes of the participants changing, must have been re-enacted along the length of the Pilgrims' Way since history began.

IT is a sad fact that it is difficult today to travel the Pilgrims' Way without being made aware of man's invasion of the English countryside. The noise of trains, traffic and aeroplanes is constant, and twentieth century eyesores are commonplace.

Elizabeth Harris showing one of the handmade quilts which she and her talented team of needlewomen make to traditional designs at Otford.

But it is still just possible to picture the cheerful people described in this poem, *The Pilgrimage*:

> 'Oh merry men, who come this way
> All through the golden meadows;
> And journey with the sun each day
> Into the evening shadows.
> With scrip and shoon and jangling bell
> And hearts with laughter flowing;
> May fortune smile and bless full well
> Your coming and your going.'

THE WEALD

IT is hard to find any two people who can agree on the exact extent of the Kent and Sussex Weald. Called Andredsweald by the Anglo-Saxon invaders it was a densely forested area stretching from the North to the South Downs. Today it is a region of orchards and hop-gardens, of corn and beef, of commuters and motor cars. It is a place described by Rudyard Kipling:

'Here through the long, unhampered days
The tinkling silence thrills;
Or little, lost Down churches praise
The Lord who made the hills;
And here the old gods guard their round
And, in her secret heart,
The heathen kingdom Wilfrid found
Dreams as she dwells apart.'

In 1803 the canal engineer, John Rennie, described the Weald as 'almost destitute of practicable roads – the interior untraversed except by bands of smugglers'. And, writing as recently as 1923, Donald Maxwell claimed that the Weald is 'a wilderness impenetrable by man or beast'.

The only obstacle nowadays is the rich and heavy clay soil, which the Wealden farmers love. In addition to fertile crops, this earth has also nourished magnificent oaks, long considered the very best for Tudor ship-building and for the elegant, beamed houses. The dense and impassable woods were virtually destroyed over the course of a couple of centuries, because of the discovery of iron deposits beneath the Weald. The woodland was decimated to fuel the fires of the iron forges. Archbishop Parker wrote in alarm to Queen Elizabeth I about the growth of ironworks in the area and the inroads made by the iron-masters on the woods and forests for fuel. Earlier, in the first year of the Queen's reign, alarmists succeeded in having an Act passed which provided that 'timber should not be felled to make coals for burning iron within fourteen miles of the sea or of the river Thames'; but this prohibition was not to extend to any part of Sussex, nor to the Weald of Kent, nor to the neighbouring parishes of Charlewood, Newdigate and Leigh in the Weald of Surrey.

61

Soon more laws were passed to prevent this grave danger to Britain's maritime supremacy. Michael Drayton recalls this period:

'Jove's oak, the warlike ash, veined elm, the softer beech,
Short hazel and smooth birch must altogether burn;
What should the builder serve supplies the forger's turn,
When under public good, base private gain takes hold
And we, poor woeful woods, to ruin lastly sold.'

Historians have wondered whether the outcome of the Battle of Hastings would have been different if Harold and his forces had retreated through the Weald, and lured William the Conqueror into a region without roads and without food. When the Saxons held the south coast the British retreated into the forest of the Weald. The invaders dug themselves in and fortified the South Downs. They refused to be tempted into the wilderness and, eventually, according to Saxon accounts, the British were exterminated.

THERE is still enough fine wood left in the Weald for the needs of Reg Saunders and his team of skilled craftsmen at Herstmonceux. They mould and construct trugs – beautifully-shaped baskets – for sale in this country and across the world. In old sheds, full of the smell of wood and steam, they ply their skilful trade with amazing old tools and benches. 'I was born and bred in this part of the world. I started at Netherfield, then I moved to Lindfield, then on to Hoo, next to Ashburnham close to Battle and, last of all to Herstmonceux. And here I stay.'

Reg sits astride an old wooden shaving-horse and planes the long strips of wood down to thin and pliable shapes. Outside, as the afternoon light begins to fade, a fresh load of timber arrives on a land rover. In a separate building two men begin to trim the logs down to manageable size. In spite of a painful limp and the December chill, Reg still gets pleasure out of the job. 'I don't feel too bad at the moment but when I do come to die, I want my ashes sprinkled where I used to play right-back for Herstmonceux up on the football pitch. I played for the village for twenty-four years up to when I got the old leg shot up. There's not many of us left trugging now. I've only got a couple of years to go – God being willing – and I am going to enjoy most of it. Trouble is that you can't get youngsters to come into it. You just can't.'

Reg is a tough, slim man with a fierce face and an abrupt manner, which can soften dramatically when he smiles. He has a way with wood, which comes from years of working with it, but also from an instinct which was born in him. 'We use sweet chestnut, which is very good. It's not difficult to get. It comes from Ashford and different parts of Sussex. The willow's the difficulty. It's hard to come by now. Then you must cure it properly, which is all part of trug-making, and you cleave it, and leave it for about six months. Just how long depends on the sun in the spring. If it's a bright spring it's OK and it seasons quickly. If it's a poor spring, well, it takes

The countryside in winter has its own particular beauty, as shown in this photograph taken at Charing Heath near Ashford.

The small pearl-bordered fritillary butterfly can be seen in woodland clearings from June–September, though they will settle on grassy paths in overcast weather. This one was photographed near Littlebredy in Dorset.

longer. But then, afterwards, you put it away in the dry and the bark stays on.'

At one end of the long shed a tall man, wearing a blue French beret, moves silently back and forward between two long steam ovens. As he pulls the strips out of the steam he bends them round a piece of wood and nails them securely before hanging them above his head. The circles he has made are the rims of the various trugs in all their different shapes and sizes. 'We got a chap named Tony Ransome, who's been here thirty-seven years. He's deaf and dumb, but a fantastic craftsman. Before Tony gets the wood I shave it up on the old shaving-horse and get it into shape. Then I take it out to Tony, who puts it in the steamer and then nails it into a rim round a former.' Tony's sensitive face is placid as he works. There is economy and smoothness in all his movements. Around the beams, which support the corrugated tin roof, some ivy has fought its way in from the outside and is now growing healthily in the warm, damp atmosphere. It decorates the rims of the trugs as Tony hangs them upon the beams.

At the other end of the building, close beside the area where great cartwheels of finished trugs are on display, and where customers come to buy their baskets, a cheerful housewife hammers away at the frames and adds slats to make the body of the trugs. She works deftly and with great speed. But, since the baskets have a reputation for long life, she must also work with care and vigilance. 'We've got an old party up the other end called Barbara. She's been here more than a year or two. She nails it all up and makes the frame. Because you've got to have it rigid. And then, having done that, if she's not doing her housework or looking after the grand-children, she makes the finished trugs.'

There's a strong feeling of commitment in the workshop, created by people who take a pride in what they are doing. There is also a sense of importance and self-respect, created by a belief that they are all ambassadors for Britain. 'I would have said that 75% of our market is overseas at the moment. Possibly it's because the dollar's so low that the Yanks are buying them up left, right and centre. And it's keeping us going. It's good, because we've got something they haven't got. I'm doin' overtime now and raking in a bit of beer money, so I'm laughin' all the way to the bank. But it's good value too. I mean, what can you buy for a tenner that's going to last you twenty-five or thirty years. You buy a pair of shoes or a pair of trousers, a frying pan or whatever – it don't last.' Outside the winter moon shines brightly in the cold sky, but the work continues apace and the sound of saws biting into wood echoes into the dark, surrounding fields.

THE pride of the Weald are the herds of slow, red Sussex cattle, which graze the rich pastures. Solid as teak, they were once used to pull the carts and the wagons at harvest-time. Today, they provide some of the country's finest beef. Bob Isted is the busy stockman at Hurlingham Farm at Brede. As he trudges through the clay with a hay-bale on his back, he is full of admiration for his precious charges. 'Where other breeds have got to be fed hard, the Sussex on this ground and on these marshes, they just manage to do on nothing. For most of them it's too heavy a ground to leave them out all the year round down here. They've got to come in in winter. They originate from the draft oxen, and they used to pull the ploughs. They were work animals, and on this heavy land they had to be pretty powerful, which means a lot of muscle, which means a lot of beef.'

Great covered yards of young stock monopolise the farmyard. Bob empties bags of crushed corn into troughs and the shaggy heads pop out one at a time as he passes by. Nearby are stalls with mother cows and their newborn calves. On the wall are the rosettes and cards from some of the top agricultural shows, where his cattle have won prizes. Outside, in two pens that look built to house elephants, stand the sires of the herd – two mighty red bulls, which seem as placid as donkeys. 'They're really docile, you know. A quiet temperament. They're a wonderful breed compared to the big Continental cattle that are in this country now. But for me, it doesn't much matter what breed they are. They've all got their place. These ones have their place as marvellous crossing animals and butchers' beasts. They've got minds too, you know. Like all animals, if you treat them nice they're all right.' And, with that piece of wisdom, Bob disappears into the yard to look after his herd, his old cap at a jaunty angle and a spring in his step.

EVEN during the dreariest winter week, Martin Woodcock from Staplehurst is out and about looking for and sketching the birds of the Weald. Clad in a dark blue balaclava helmet and the warmest of raincoats he stands out in the worst weather for hours at a time, his eagle eye scanning the hedgerows and the fields of sheep for lapwings, fieldfares, pigeons or rooks. His skilled and creative work is to paint pictures of every kind of bird for book illustrations and for framing. As he works in the wild wind his sketchbook is filled with pictures, which will be transferred onto paper or canvas when he gets back to his warm home. 'I've always lived in the Weald. I was educated at the far end, where the clay is about four hundred feet deeper than it is here. So I've had my feet in clay all my life. I like it here. In fact, I love it.'

Man's attachment to a place or an area is one of the oldest and strongest instincts, which is being destroyed by the modern mania for moving about and moving on. Martin feels no such urge. 'Ever since I was strong enough to pick up a pencil I've had one in my hand. For years and years it made quite irrational lines on the paper, and I'm just beginning to tame it a bit now. In my line of country I suppose that the most obvious and typical birds are the farmland birds like lapwings, starlings and wood pigeons, which you get in quite big flocks in the open fields. And also, in certain places, rooks and jackdaws. Then there are the birds of the hedges – yellow-hammers, linnets and those sort of things – which are characteristic of the area, but they're not quite so obvious as the big flocks of lapwings. It may seem to be a statement of great simplicity, but just because a bird is a common type does not mean it is not beautiful and cannot make a good picture.'

The eyes do not smile as they observe. The nose points like a compass needle. The big body is tense. Only the hand seems relaxed as it brushes across the paper and the sketch fills out and grows. 'I suppose it's an inspiration. You look at some birds in a hedge and you think you must paint that. For instance, with the fieldfares that feed in bunches on the red berries in the hedges at this time of the year – the white underwing, the grey rumps and the lovely, dull red of the hawthorns all say "picture" in my mind. And then, when I get back home, I have to go through the quite difficult task of redrawing them, getting them in the right positions, moving them around on the paper until I arrive at some sort of composition. And sometimes, even then, they don't work.'

Back at Martin's house there is all the confusion of an artist at work. Paint everywhere, sketches lying on desks and tables, bowls of lovely feathers, jars of paint brushes, open books, easels, tubes of paint. In addition, there is silence, apart from the sound of pencil on paper and the distant barking of a dog across the meadows. 'One of the things that has always been a very important feature to me is the whole idea of a bird being in its bush, on its field or in the water. The creature and its environment or setting are inseparable to me, and I'm learning to try to express this in paint, which is a very difficult thing to achieve. Some parts have to be sharp and in focus. Other parts you have to soften. And it's very good working with twigs and branches because you've got interesting shapes to work with, which helps a lot.'

Across the room there is an oil painting under way of a pheasant soaring skywards at a steep angle. To give himself a break from the sketching and the water colours Martin Woodcock moves over to the easel, picks up his palette and starts mixing colours, so that he can do some more work on the heavy, green undergrowth. 'I don't know that I've ever seen a photo of a cock pheasant springing up out of the bracken. The day before I started to paint this picture I had two of them do it under my nose just up the hill, and it was very convenient and obliging of them. So I had a good visual impression then and that's all I really need to go on. Add to that the fact that we have kind friends who supply us with pheasants from time to time, which helps of course, and I shall be using those too. It's a new dimension; looking forward to eating something you have just painted is an amazing sensation.'

KENT would claim to grow the best hops in the world, and the Weald is covered by hop-gardens. Oast houses are seldom used for their original purpose nowadays. More often they are the homes of wealthy commuters. But they are still crowned by their traditional white wooden cowls. David Holmes from East Peckham runs one of the few remaining businesses in the area which specialises in building and repairing oast-house cowls. The yard outside his workshop looks like a view of Easter Island or some savage cemetery, as the wooden pinnacles stand waiting to be worked on or to be restored to their former positions of glory. 'From new, they might last seventy or eighty years – even a hundred. It all depends on the timber you can get to build them, really. You have to take them down and work on them every eight to ten

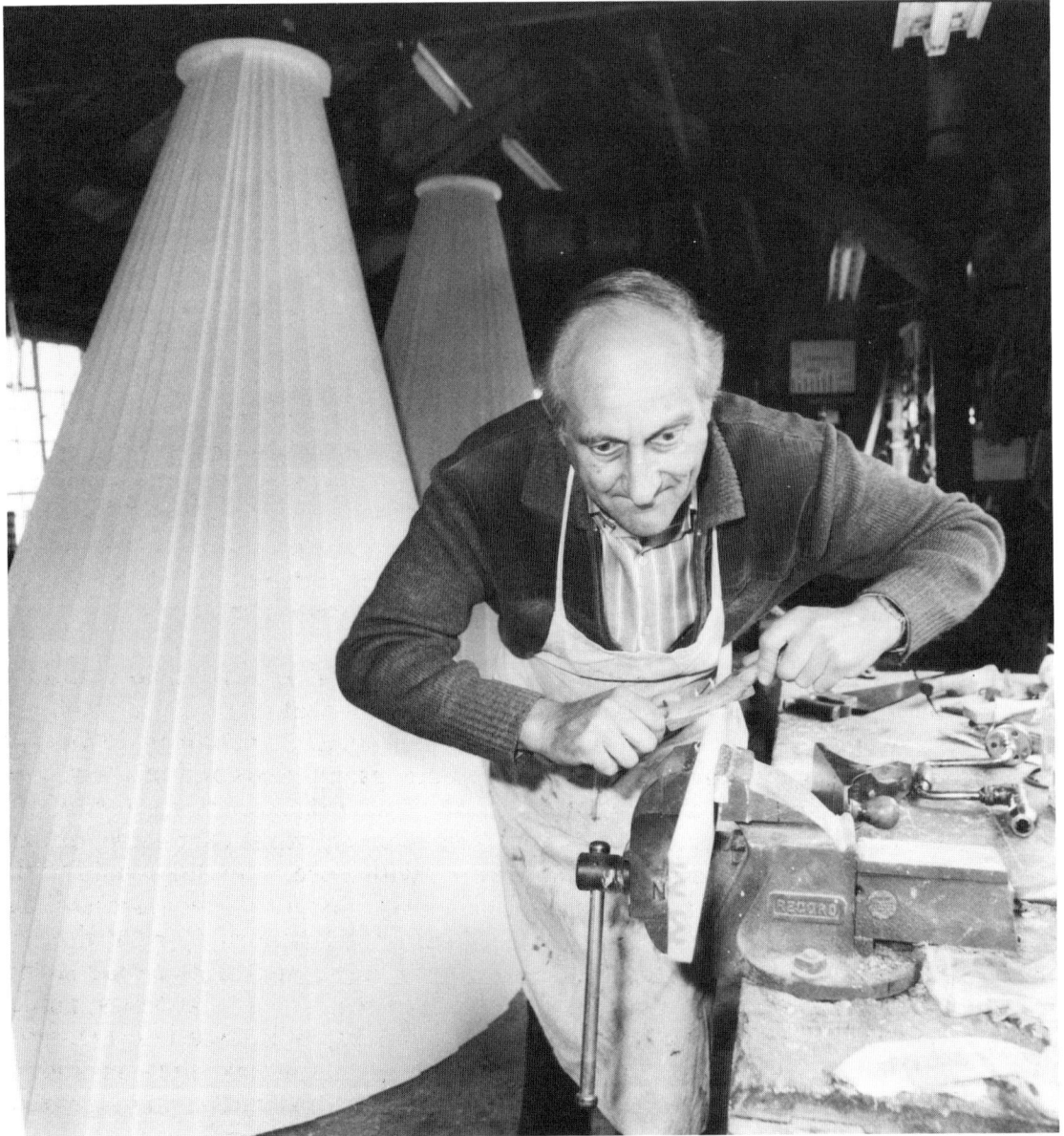

David Holmes from East Peckham runs one of the few remaining businesses building and repairing the traditional white wooden cowls so distinctive of oast houses in the hop-growing area of the Weald.

years. You clean them and repaint them – two undercoats and two gloss coats. If you do that regularly they have a good life span.'

At an oast nearby there is frantic activity and much shouting and calling, echoed and repeated by a flock of startled geese. The cowl is being taken down. A long, wooden pole stretches from the top of the roof. On the lawn David is hanging onto a rope and taking the strain with one of his employees. Up on the roof a shaggy, blonde head pops out of the hole left by the cowl and watches as it bumps its way slowly down. But for the movement of the eyes you could imagine the head stuck on the end of a spear – some grisly, mediaeval topping-out ceremony. 'Some of these cowls are very heavy. We have to use a winch to get them down. But, as far as most of them go, it's all done basically with a pole. You erect the pole at the top of the kiln, swing the cowl off on the pole and then lower it to the ground. Sounds easy and usually is. But not every time.'

Back at the workshop with its earth floor covered in wood-shavings and debris, the cowls lie on their sides looking like beached rowing-boats. The men work away at that steady speed which only countrymen know, and which eats up the job and allows them to keep going without continual breaks for tea or reflection. It is 'more hurry, less speed' in action. 'It is like boat-building in a way, and especially looks like it when the cowl is lying upside down. Like a boat you have to chamfer the edges of the boards and then taper them so that they go round in a circle without buckling. That's the reason they are done like that. It's a shame that we don't do many now for drying hops. It's mostly for conversions into houses. But at least it pleases the architects. They go mad, because they're such fantastic buildings inside.'

PARTICULARLY in winter the Weald may appear to be flat, heavy land with little obvious interest. But become familiar with it and it will offer you a wealth of scenery and wildlife, and a fascinating variety of buildings. As you drop down onto the clay from the high ground in the north there are distant views and mist-wrapped churches, which remain etched on your memory. Like other country areas, winter sees the Weald at its quietest. Empty oast houses stand sentinel over ranks of bare hop-poles, arranged on weed-free parade grounds with a precision that would be the envy of any regimental sergeant major. The grassy pastures, which are still the predominant feature of Wealden farming, remain dotted with sheep right through the cold months. But these damp meadows also provide a vital winter food supply for other creatures, and particularly for the birds of the Weald – lapwings, golden plovers, moorhens, tree-creepers, goldfinches, dunnocks, gulls, thrushes, fieldfares, tits and even common-or-garden starlings. And, for those who take the time and the trouble to use their eyes, the birds will add another bonus to the many physical beauties which await any explorer of this ancient part of England.

THE HOO PENINSULA

THE Hoo Peninsula sits in the mouth of the Thames, just upstream of the Isle of Sheppey. The word 'Hoo' means 'spur' and, like Plymouth Hoe in the West Country, it pushes its snub-nosed way out into the water from the mainland. In 1948 Richard Church described Hoo as 'cut off from the mainstream of life'. He said that it offered 'space and silence and solitude' to those in search of peace.

At first sight, this northernmost part of Kent is not an ideal place for a rest cure — particularly during a bleak and bitter winter. To the north is Canvey Island with its massive oil storage tanks and unwelcoming shoreline. The eastern flank is the Isle of Grain with its power station and industrial debris. The motorway networks and Kingsnorth Power Station lie to the south. The Dartford tunnel, the Thames barrier and then the outskirts of London are close by in the east. Across the landscape giant pylons march in all directions and chalk and gravel pits scar its marshy surface. But in spite of all these horrors, you can find on the Peninsula a heronry to compete with any in the world; some wonderfully wild and desolate marshland full of waterfowl and wildlife, and some superb farming land where top-rate vegetables and fruit are grown to the highest standards.

The Hoo Peninsula is also Charles Dickens country. He loved it dearly and set some of his most dramatic scenes here. *Great Expectations* begins in the churchyard at Cooling — an isolated spot close to the fourteenth-century castle, which was built to defend the estuary from the French. It was here that the terrifying convict leapt out on poor Pip from behind the gravestones. In the same graveyard there is a group of thirteen tiny tombs — a complete family wiped out in the 1770s by some plague or mosquito-borne disease of the Hoo marshes. In his book Dickens only had five of Pip's family die in infancy, but the tragic tiny memorials in Cooling were his inspiration. And the area is full of melancholy and mystery, which must have been even more evident when the writer went there in the middle of the last century.

ALAN Parker, slim, shy and bespectacled, lives in the back of beyond at Swiggs Hole Cottage, High Halstow. To the north the flat fields stretch away to the sea wall along the estuary. But it is not all marsh. Behind Alan's home is a ridge of low, clay, wooded hills, which runs east of Higham to High Halstow and then drops down to the Thames at All Hallows. Alan is in charge of a magnificent heronry which fills the woods with the honking of the birds and the skies above with their strong and graceful flight patterns. He also takes care of thousands of geese, waders and wildfowl, which visit the Hoo Peninsula in all seasons. He seems to relish the isolation and the loneliness, and he enjoys the contrasts between his patch of wilderness and the surrounding, industrial scene.

'It certainly seems to be a bleak and barren old place, especially on a cold and grey winter's day. But, if you're interested in birds, it's a very good place to be at the moment, even though it is quite close to London. This is really the best time for geese, ducks and waders, and there are thousands of birds to be seen out there just by wandering along the sea wall. Of course, the landscape around here has changed considerably over the centuries. There would have been acres and acres of reeds in the past with sheep and some cattle grazing everywhere, and there would have been pools of water and lots of ducks. Now it's drained and planted up with wheat and almost all the birds are on the other side of the sea wall. What is quite interesting to realise is that the river is now very much better than it was. It's now quite a clean river and there's impressive bird-watching there at any time of the year.'

As Alan looks out across the marshland a great cloud of large birds comes flying in from the water, trumpeting their arrival. They land confidently on the rich soil where the winter corn is beginning to show. 'The Brent geese that are here now rather like eating wheat, and they cause one or two problems in that way. We get white-fronted geese too. But it's not a good breeding-ground for waders and ducks. So at least the farmers are spared visits from them. In the summer, of course, it's very different. But it's less interesting for me then. I suppose the notable breeding birds would be yellow wagtails – probably the most obvious breeding bird out in these sort of fields. In what is left of the grazing marsh there are redshanks, some shovellers, lapwings and mallards. But it's not a great area for breeding birds. There's some remaining sticks of reed left in the fleets and in the ditches, and we do have one or two interesting things, like bearded tits. But it's very much a remnant of what would have been here once.'

Alan uses a motorbike to travel round his territory. Many of the tracks are rough and muddy, and there is no space for a wider vehicle. High in the woods he clears and burns brush and brambles while herons fly back and forth and, in the distance, a cargo ship hoots as it heads upstream towards Tilbury and Gravesend. Below, the flatlands stretch out to the Thames with an isolated building here and there breaking the smooth surface of the marsh. 'This is *the* woodland for this area and it draws in all the woodland birds for miles around. We've got large populations of warblers and turtle-doves and a good population of nightingales. With 230 pairs, the heronry is the biggest in Britain. I suppose it's not surprising that it's here, when you think that it's a protected woodland next to such a large area of marsh. The fields down there have good ditches in between them, and there are still plenty of eels and fishing beetles and so on for the herons to eat. And that's clearly the reason that it's such a good heronry.'

Alan Parker is in charge of the heronry near High Halstow. He also takes care of the many migrant geese, waders and wildfowl which visit the Hoo Peninsula.

The woods are full of rabbits and pheasants. In a quiet moment a big dog-fox clambers up the slope from the trees where the herons are building their nests. Although birds are his main preoccupation, Alan has time for other creatures as well. 'We have a good range of butterflies. We get up to thirty species. On a good day you should be able to see at least twenty kinds, which is really quite impressive. They include white-letter hair-streak, which depends on elm trees and which has suffered because of Dutch Elm disease. Through good fortune and, I hope, good management we've got a lot of these butterflies where we're growing elms. This is the only site in Kent and possibly the best place in Britain for them, so we're very much aware of them and looking after them is part of my work.'

If you ask Alan to choose between the woodland and the marsh he is stuck for an answer. The truth is that he loves and jealously guards both. 'If you know where to look and you look hard enough you'll find something to see in both places at all times of the year. The wood in winter can seem fairly quiet as you walk around it. But if you're there at first light or at dusk when the birds are leaving or coming in to roost, it's alive. Thousands of pigeons and collar doves, a large number of rooks and jackdaws all wheeling around making lots of noise; winter thrushes, field-fare, redwings and finches — all piling in from all directions. And, of course, they attract the odd birds of prey as well. It's surprising that the merlin is the commonest bird of prey here on Northwood Hill. It's usually thought of as a fairly remote upland type or from the large marshes, but it's in here every day after the linnets and the other small birds that are roosting. I think that as I do a lot of work in the wood all winter to try and make it a better habitat, May is my favourite month, because that is when you start seeing the results of what you have done. Berries that have been dead and brown all winter suddenly become green, and everything starts leaping about and singing. And it makes it all worthwhile. But it can be a bit tricky living out on the marsh in the winter.'

And the lonely figure pitchforks the bracken and brambles onto the bonfire and, as dusk closes in, the woodsmoke drifts upwards through the bare branches of the trees towards the evening sky.

THERE are many surprises on the Hoo Peninsula. One of them is that this is hunting country. It is served by the West Kent Hunt, which comes up from Penshurst. And there is splendid, flat marshland for horses and riders to gallop over. Resplendent in hunting pink, farmer Tim Lyle is the senior joint master. One of the places where they regularly meet is at Oakleigh Farm, Lower Higham. Here fruit is king and strawberries cover acres of the dark earth. 'The West Kent Hunt is kennelled at my farm over at Penshurst. We hunt two days a week on Tuesdays and Saturdays and we have about eighty subscribers. We have a waiting list because the enthusiasm for all horse-sports is on the increase. But we have to keep our field down to a maximum of eighty, because we do too much damage on the farmland if we have more than that. The interesting thing about hunting up this end of our area on the marsh is that it's open country and you can see the hounds working. You can watch them hunting all day. Whereas the other part of the country, the Kent/Sussex border, where I farm, is very wooded. You can hear the sounds all right, but it's very difficult to see them. So it's good to come up into an open place where you can actually watch hounds at work.'

The big horses clatter down from the boxes. They look aloof and superior, and they shine with health and grooming. An avalanche of hounds pours out of a nearby trailer, baying and barking and wagging their tails. A beautiful and mysterious woman with a top hat and black veil mounts side-saddle with dignity and elegance, and the huntsmen begin to gather the hounds together. 'There are enormous numbers of foxes up here. They're on the increase. I know in this part of Kent they're not terribly keen on them, because it's a very intensive pheasant-shooting area. But we're never short of foxes. Our main trouble in the winter is if we get ice. The horses are valuable and you can't risk having them slip and breaking a leg. But, whatever the conditions, we get a wonderful welcome on the Hoo Peninsula. They're always pleased to see us, and it makes the journey over here well worthwhile.'

In front of the farmhouse generous stirrup-cups are handed up to the riders. Small children walk fearlessly among the hounds and horses. And a flurry of hail rattles the window-panes of the old house. The huntsman sounds his horn and they move off towards the water meadows.

A distant horn sounds and hounds and horses thunder across a green field, while startled birds spring out of the hedges and divots fly in all directions.

THERE are not many outdoor games that you would want to play for pleasure in the pouring rain on a freezing January evening on the Hoo Peninsula. Certainly, cricket would be out of the question. But the hard and dedicated villagers of Upper Stoke are willing to demonstrate their skill at a far older game, said to have been one of the origins of cricket, on the foulest imaginable winter's night. The game is called Bat and Trap. Picture, if you will, a strip of grass outside a welcoming pub called The White Horse Inn. It is pitch dark. The rain is beginning to turn to snow. At one end a group of villagers, with umbrellas and pints, stand huddled together in the spotlights while one of their number takes the bat (a sort of king-sized butter-pat) approaches the trap, knocks a hard rubber ball in the air and whacks it between two boundary lines towards another group of villagers at the far end. All is well provided that the ball stays within the boundary lines and that you do not get caught. The bowler returns the ball underarm and tries to knock down a small hinged flap at the base of the batsman's position. If the flap is struck the batsman is out. Otherwise he picks up the ball and has another turn. Easy, isn't it?

One of these eccentric enthusiasts is farm worker Len Andrews, who lives in the village. 'We generally play from May to September in the summer time. They say the game started six hundred years ago. Locally, it began in Canterbury about 1500. And they do say that cricket was based on Bat and Trap.' Len is big and bulky and pink of face with a favourite cap perched on the back of his head. He speaks softly with the slow drawl of northern Kent, which proximity to London has done nothing to tame. His eyes are bright and the game is important to him. 'The principle of it is that the bowler tries to hit the wicket. If he succeeds you're out. But you can also be caught by the bowler if he has one foot behind the base line. Or you can be out by the ball going over the lines down the side. And if none of those things happens and you hit the ball straight and true you get a run. It's a bit more difficult than it may look, I can tell you. One of the good things about the game is that men and women play together. It seems to me that you don't get the bitterness that you do when it's all men. And another good thing about these teams is that we're all local lads. There's none comes from anywhere outside the Peninsula.'

There is the same loyalty and brotherhood here as there seems to be in all ancient, close-knit communities. As the players sit steaming and laughing in the pub after the game, there is an atmosphere of security and old-fashioned togetherness. 'I've lived here all me life. I've worked on the farm in this village. That's what holds me here. That and the friendship. It's a bit bleak in the winter, especially when the wind's out the east way. Yeah, but you put up with that, 'cos it keeps your lungs clean.' And with his broad back drying out in front of a blazing fire Len looks right at home.

THE Church of St. Mary Magdalene at Cobham contains some of the finest mediaeval brasses in the world. Thrown out by Cromwell's men, they were found over a hundred years later bundled up in a chest from which local workmen were systematically stealing them. They were re-laid in the Church in 1837 to the delight of today's vicar, Peter Thomson.

'They started building the church in about 1200, and the brasses date from the 14th century. They've had a bit of a chequered history since then. They were originally made to honour the people from the local big houses – the Brookes and the de Cobhams. Cromwell made a bad choice, because whoever he sent down to destroy the brasses and the other church ornaments seems to have been related in some way to these powerful families. He just hid the brasses away round the corner, hoping that the tide would turn and that he'd then be able to pull them out again. So we're really very lucky to have them still.'

It was an 18th century traveller who found the hidden treasures and discovered that they were being taken away by thieves. As a result, nobody knows how many brasses there originally were. It seems likely that the stolen ones were melted down and turned into bullets in the munitions factory at Chatham, though it is just conceivable that they lie buried in some village garden or, more likely perhaps, beneath the foundations of the M2. Wherever they may be, the ones that remain have attracted many famous people to the lovely church.

'I can't vouch for this story, but I've heard that Lawrence of Arabia was very keen on getting the brasses, and he wasn't allowed to rub them. So one winter's afternoon he crept in and hid under a pew. When the church was locked up he set to work and got a complete set of rubbings. He then hid under the pew again until the church was open next morning and crept away.'

ST. Mary's is a Mecca for brass rubbing enthusiasts from around the world. Cyril Barnard, who lives in Cobham, makes sure that they do it properly, and that they get good results. Stretched out on the ice-cold floor, he rubs steadily and cautiously at a long scroll of paper with his thick piece of heel-ball – an old-fashioned cobbler's recipe made from wax and lampblack. 'I think the fascination is that it is something you've accomplished yourself – your own work of art. It's also marvellous to be working on something very old and historic, and you can take the results home with you. People come into the church and they're overjoyed. Then you realise what a privilege it is to be here, and sometimes to be able to help them, though, of course, many of them are already good at it. You also get people who have never done brass rubbing before, and that's always rewarding.'

Slowly the figure begins to emerge on the paper as the skill of the old artist is transferred from metal to paper. 'The way to describe it is to remind people of when they were children, and they used to rub on a coin with a pencil and paper. It's more difficult than that, of course, because the brasses are much bigger. You've got to go very carefully and to have sensitive fingers, so that you can feel the outlines under the rubbing paper. You need patience too. It's no good rushing it if you want a good result. You just have to go ahead firmly and gently.' The silence of the church is broken only by the soft rubbing of stick on paper, like the sound of mice moving behind a skirting board.

JUST up the Thames from the Hoo Peninsula is the turmoil of the area around the entrance to the Dartford tunnel. It is not a pretty sight. Roads criss-cross in all directions. Seagulls swarm over a mournful rubbish tip. Earth-movers do their dirty work. And, if you are not careful, you can get swept along under the Thames by the relentless traffic heading north. But there is an oasis of rural calm in the midst of the surrounding nightmare. It is Stone Lodge Farm Park, where Colin Barber and his energetic team keep alive the old countryside in all its forms. Here you will find horse-ploughing and oxen, an old threshing machine in action, an ancient working forge, and lambs and piglets and calves and geese and all the fun of the farmyard. 'It seems to be a style that everybody wants to see these days. They want to turn the clock back. On modern farms the gates are being closed and everything's become intensified. But people want to see horses working, and they like to look at the rare breeds that would become extinct if they weren't looked after. Obviously it's hard work and a tractor would be a godsend at times. But it's still very satisfying.'

As Colin ploughs straight furrows with two heavy horses at the far end of the farm, the sound of industry and traffic engulfs him. It is a study in contrasts as the old skills are carried on to the sound of modern machinery. 'In a strange way it sets everything off if you can see industry at work from a farm where we've gone back to the 1890s. There's quite a lot of people now that are teaching the skills of working horses. And there are some youngsters too, who are learning to break them in. Harness makers are coming back, and farriers. It's a revival of everything to do with the heavy horse. As far as the ploughing goes it's a very easy harness with chains running along the sides of the horses. You have to teach them what to do to start with – one to walk in the furrow and one to walk on the land. It's just practice and perseverance. You've got to keep going and, if it doesn't work right, then you alter your harness till it does go right. It's a matter of trial and error. It's also a job without any hassle. It's hard work but it's very, very rewarding.'

Colin is optimistic enough to believe that there is still a future for cart-horses in farming. 'They're coming back, that's for sure. They're playing a part in small forms of agriculture and haulage – even forestry. People are finding that horses can haul trees from the forest easier than a machine, and they don't do the damage. Oh yes, they're coming back in quite a large way.'

During the spring, summer and autumn the farm is open to the public, and they come in their hundreds from the towns for a breath of country air. 'They will come back week in and week out to see how the litters are getting on and to see how quickly they're growing. And, if we're expecting a birth, we let people know and they'll come back every day if they have to, determined to see the litter or a foal being born. They come back until they've seen it. And then they'll go on coming back to find out how the young ones are getting on.'

Chicks are hatching in an incubator in an old wooden shed. An imperial Dorset Horn ram looks proudly across the valley from the hillside, his mighty horns silhouetted against the grey sky. A cloud of doves circles and settles on the roof of the barn. And the cattle munch the hay in the covered yards. All round them the modern world throbs and roars.

A SHORT way to the south of the Hoo Peninsula at Nurstead Hill Farm, Longfield, David and Dorothy Broomfield run their flourishing Longfield Carriage Company. They make it possible for Motorway Mad drivers to travel at a safer speed in the old and elegant style in shining landaus and broughams, drawn by handsome Welsh cobs. The collection of beautifully kept carriages is sheltered in a big barn at the back. The farmyard itself, a tumult of dogs, cats, harness, helpers, horses and buckets, is a hive of activity as they prepare to exercise and train horses and drivers along the narrow Kent lanes.

'Mostly the horses come from North Wales and it's taken us a long time to find matching pairs. We've got nine carriages including the hearse, which has to be drawn by a pair of black cobs, of course. It's getting difficult to find good carriages now. They're becoming scarcer and scarcer. In the summer we're out most weekends for weddings, and there are quite a number of people now who have asked for them for their funerals. It's usually people that have lived with horses all their lives and then think that they'd like to go on their last journey in the traditional style. And I think that sort of thing is on the increase. Of course, we spend a lot of time training the horses. They have to be as good as a police horse, because they have to put up with the same traffic and the same kind of problems.'

On the quiet back-roads the carriages show above the hedges as they make their stately way along. It is a sight with which Charles Dickens would have felt quite at

The grey heron stands over three feet tall. It will stand completely motionless in water and then stab suddenly at fish, eels and even frogs.

home in his ramblings through North Kent. He would also have enjoyed one of David Broomfield's wedding stories. 'There was this village with several churches in it. We were new to the place and we took the bride to the wrong church, where there was another wedding going on. The bride and her father just sat in the carriage and never said a word. And the usher came out to us, opened the door, looked inside and said, "She's either too early or too late. But she's not ours!" And he slammed the door again. So we had to trot off very quickly along to the next church!'

IT is not glamorous country on the Hoo Peninsula, but the local people are intensely and touchingly loyal to it. They have an eloquent supporter in Charles Dickens, who described it through the eyes of Pip on the first page of *Great Expectations*. 'Ours was the marsh country down by the river within, as the river wound, twenty miles of the sea. My first most vivid and broad impression of the identity of things seems to me to have been gained on a memorable raw afternoon towards evening. I found out then for certain . . . that the dark, flat wilderness beyond the churchyard, intersected with dykes and mounds and gates, with scattered cattle feeding on it, was the marshes; and that the low leaden line beyond was the river; and that the distant, savage lair, from which the wind was rushing, was the sea; and that the small bundle of shivers growing afraid of it all and beginning to cry, was Pip.'

INDEX